WITTGENSTEIN AND HIS TIMES

Anthony Kenny, Brian McGuinness
J. C. Nyíri, Rush Rhees
and G. H. von Wright

edited by
Brian McGuinness

Basil Blackwell · Oxford

First published 1982
Basil Blackwell Publisher Limited
108 Cowley Road, Oxford OX4 1JF, England

British Library Cataloguing in Publication Data

Wittgenstein and his times.
1. Wittgenstein, Ludwig
I. McGuinness, Brian
192   B3376.W564

ISBN 0-631-11161-1

Printed in Great Britain
at The Blackwell Press Limited,
Guildford, London, Oxford, Worcester.

Contents

Editor's Preface

These papers have been collected because they seemed to illustrate a common theme (not necessarily envisaged by each several author), namely that of the agreement and difference between Wittgenstein's thought and the thought of some who were in a broad sense his contemporaries. That he did both have features in common with and react against a number of such thinkers is unsurprising, though it has not always been remarked. More striking is the extent to which he was ahead of his time, so that problems he dealt with are only now becoming clear to us or have yet (supposing them real) to do so. He sometimes showed that he expected this.

These papers may also be seen — it is indeed another aspect of the same point — as amounting to an attempt to tease out Wittgenstein's central or characteristic attitude, his Weltanschauung, by concentrating on areas where he seems nearest to contradiction, because, perhaps, there is most tension in his thought. Wittgenstein seems like a conservative thinker, though his political sympathies were often progressive; he seems to condemn psychoanalysis, yet he practised something very like it; he exposes the weaknesses of traditional philosophies by a method which is itself a subtly differentiated form of traditional philosophy. Perhaps — the Wittgensteinian may think and the reader must judge — the point is that these are contradictions only when viewed from a pre-Wittgensteinian standpoint. If we could acquire his concepts, win through to his way of looking at things, the contradictions would vanish. Mr Rhees's paper here is the clearest attempt to make that breakthrough in a certain area: he has handselled others elsewhere.

But enough of this apologia, which should no more be too long than be omitted altogether. The editor can speak only for himself; better that the book should speak for itself. The idea of it arose in the course of the Symposium of the Wittgenstein Archiv held at Tübingen in 1977 as part of the quincentennial celebrations of that university. There the consilience of the public lectures given by Dr Kenny, Mr Rhees, and myself was remarked. Professor von Wright proved open to persuasion that his opening address for another Wittgenstein Symposium (at Kirchberg am Wechsel, Lower Austria, in 1977) belonged with them and Professor Nyíri prepared a longer version of the paper he too gave at Kirchberg.

The collection has been published in German with the title *Wittgensteins geistige Erscheinung* (Suhrkamp, Frankfurt, 1979). My colleagues Professor H. J. Heringer and Mr M. Nedo presented the material slightly differently and with a different preface. Mr Rhees's paper has been published before (without any translations from the German) in *Essays on Wittgenstein in Honour of G. H. von Wright* (*Acta Philosophica Fennica*, 28) and Professor von Wright's in *Wittgenstein and his Impact on Contemporary Thought* (Proceedings of the 2nd International Wittgenstein Symposium, Hölder-Pichler-Tempsky, Vienna, 1978). We are grateful to the publishers and editors of these volumes for permission to reprint and also to the holders of the copyright in Wittgenstein's unpublished writings (Professor G. E. M. Anscombe, Mr R. Rhees, and Professor G. H. von Wright) for permission to print the passages from these quoted in the first and second papers. In the present volume translations from Wittgenstein's writings are taken from previously published versions when suitable or else made by Dr Kenny (for his own paper) or the editor.

B. McG.

Wittgenstein on the Nature of Philosophy

Anthony Kenny

One of the most constant features of Wittgenstein's philosophy throughout his life, was his view of the nature of philosophy itself. In this paper I shall discuss his view of philosophy in the central period of his life, the period which began with his return to the subject of philosophy in the late 1920s. In the early thirties Wittgenstein began work on a book which at one time he gave a substantial form as what is known as the Big Typescript – a 700-page typescript divided into chapters and headed paragraphs. He was immediately dissatisfied with it; it was never meant for publication but only as a basis for publication, and he continually revised it. One of the revisions of it, edited by Rush Rhees, has been published under the title *Philosophical Grammar*. Wittgenstein continued to work at perfecting the form and content of his philosophical ideas until he died, leaving a version of his thoughts which he regarded as publishable and which is known to us as *Philosophical Investigations*. I shall concentrate on the period of Wittgenstein's life between these two books and shall be drawing on un-published parts very largely: I shall quote some familiar passages from *Philosophical Investigations* but I shall also draw partly on the Big Typescript (whose sections on philosophy do not appear in *Philosophical Grammar*) and partly on other unpublished manuscripts of the thirties.*

* I shall refer to MSS by the numbers in von Wright's "The Wittgenstein Papers", *Philosophical Review* 79 (1969), pp 483–503.

The problem from which I start is this. Wittgenstein seems at first sight to have two rather different views of philosophy. On the one hand, he often compares philosophy to a medical technique, to a therapy, a method of healing. On the other, he seems to see philosophy as giving overall understanding, a clear view of the world.

In a familiar sentence of *Philosophical Investigations* Wittgenstein says: "The philosopher's treatment of a question is like the treatment of an illness" (*PI*, I, §255). Philosophy is not a single therapy, but a set of therapies: "There is not *a* philosophical method, though there are indeed methods, like different therapies" (*PI*, I, §133). When one hears philosophy compared to a therapy, one thinks principally of psychotherapy, but Wittgenstein also thought of philosophy as being like physical medicine, as like a cure for physical diseases. He said – again I quote a familiar passage of *Philosophical Investigations*, but one written in the early thirties – "The results of philosophy are the uncovering of one or another piece of plain nonsense and of bumps that the understanding has got by running its head up against the limits of language. These bumps make us see the value of the discovery." (*PI*, I, §119, MS 213, 425) But philosophy is a medicine which is sometimes curative and sometimes preventive: a way in which it is preventive is suggested by a remark in English in his notebooks. "Philosophical questions, when you boil them down to what they really amount to, change their aspect entirely. What evaporates is what the intellect cannot take." (MS 159, 3b) The metaphor of boiling down is meant seriously: we are to think of a dietitian who has to cater to an invalid with a weak stomach, which cannot take certain foods. So the philosopher (the true philosopher) will boil down the philosophical problems so that our intellects can take them. can it?

It is especially to psychoanalysis – and to psychotherapy in general – that Wittgenstein compares his philosophy. Wittgenstein was impressed by, and critical of, the work of

Freud: he thought that his own method was a method of analysis. The comparison is made explicitly in a passage from *Philosophical Grammar*, with particular reference to the philosophy of mathematics. Wittgenstein is saying that mathematicians are very unhappy when they read what he writes on the philosophy of mathematics. They think that what he has to say is too simple, that he discusses difficulties that only a child would take seriously. Then Wittgenstein says this:

> A mathematician is bound to be horrified by my mathematical comments, since he has always been trained to avoid indulging in thoughts and doubts of the kind I develop. He has learned to regard them as something contemptible and, to use an analogy from psychoanalysis (this paragraph is reminiscent of Freud), he has acquired a revulsion from them as infantile. That is to say, I trot out all the problems that a child learning arithmetic, etc., finds difficult, the problems that education represses without solving. I say to those repressed doubts: you are quite correct, go on asking, demand clarification! (*PG*, pp. 381–382)

So, one thing that philosophical therapy involves for mathematicians, is giving expression to repressed doubts, repressed puzzlements, things that one was told not to take any notice of – "Learn mathematics, and then you won't worry any more about these doubts". This connects with a well-known saying of Wittgenstein that one of the things he wanted to do in philosophy was to turn *latent* nonsense into *patent* nonsense. When we are suffering from philosophical problems we have a bit of hidden nonsense in our minds, and the only way to cure it is to bring it out into the open. Very often, for instance, he attacks a mythology which we have about the nature of the mind. We imagine a mechanism in the mind, some strange mechanism which is capable of working very well in its own mysterious medium but which if understood as a mechanism in the ordinary sense is totally unintelligible. Wittgenstein thinks this is a bit of latent or hidden nonsense. The way to make it explicit is to imagine that mechanism really existed. You may think, for instance, that when you recognize somebody, what you do is to consult a sort of mental picture of him and check whether what you now see matches this picture. Wittgenstein suggests that if we have this nonsense picture in our mind we can make ourselves see that it is nonsense, that it in no way explains recognition. If we imagine it as happening in the real world and suppose that the picture is a real picture, on a piece of paper, the problem just returns: how do I recognize that this is a picture of a particular person in order to use it to recognize him? So this is a form of psychoanalytic therapy, in that something which is a *repressed* bit of nonsense in my mind is then made *explicit* nonsense. I give expression to it, just as in a Freudian treatment I make explicit my repressed emotions: this is part of the way of being cured of the bad results of the repression.

Another way in which the philosophical method of Wittgenstein resembles that of psychoanalysis is that in certain areas what the patient says goes, that is, the patient's acceptance of an interpretation has a specially crucial role. The patient for analysis in philosophy, of course, is the person who is suffering from a philosophical error. In philosophy in general, Wittgenstein says, there is usually no question of finding a precise description of phenomena, but if you are describing a philosophical error, you must describe it absolutely accurately; that is, the person who is under the influence of the error must say: "Yes, that's what I think, that's exactly what I think." He says: "We can bring someone's mistake home to him only when he acknowledges it as the right expression for what he feels. . . . The point is: only when he acknowledges it as such *is* it the right expression" – and then in brackets: "(Psychoanalysis)" (MS 213, 410).

The analogy between philosophy and psychoanalysis is an important and fruitful one. But rather than to develop it further, I want to ask a particular question about it. If philosophy is therapeutic – whether in the physical sense or in the psychoanalytic sense – then must not the role of philosophy be a negative one? Philosophy, it seems, is only useful to people who are sick in some way; a healthy person – a person of healthy mind and healthy body – has no need of philosophy.

This seems very different from the view of philosophy as building great systems, the traditional view of philosophy. Wittgenstein certainly agrees that philosophy has a destructive role, though he also says that what destroys is not worth preserving. There is a well-known passage in *Philosophical Investigations*:

> Where does our investigation get its importance from, since it seems only to destroy everything interesting, that is, all that is great and important? (As it were all the buildings, leaving behind only bits of stone and rubble.) What we are destroying is nothing but houses of cards, and we are clearing up the ground of language on which they stand. (*PI*, I, §118)

There is an earlier, perhaps even more vivid, expression of the same idea that philosophy is a destroyer in the Big Typescript: "All that philosophy can do is to destroy idols. And that means not making any new ones – say out of 'the absence of idols'." (MS 213, 413)

So philosophy is a destroyer of idols and of castles in the air. This view of philosophy seems to be a very negative view of philosophy, in which philosophy has only a critical role. But on the other hand, one can also find in Wittgenstein's writings evidence of what seems at first a different and more positive view of philosophy, a view of philosophy as giving a special kind of understanding, of giving a very general view of the world, an overall understanding. For instance, he says in a passage which occurs over and over again between the 1930s and the 1940s: "A main source of our failure to understand is that we do not *command a clear view* of the use of our words. Our grammar is lacking in perspicuity. . . . The concept of a perspicuous representation is of fundamental significance for us. It earmarks the form of account we give, the way we look at things" (*PI*, I, §122). And then he asks: "Is this a Weltanschauung?" and in earlier versions, in place of that question, he had said: "A sort of Weltanschauung that seems to be typical of our times. Spengler." (MS 213, 417) An early metaphor for this idea that philosophy gives us an overall view – an *Übersicht* – and how it does it, appears in a passage from the Big Typescript:

> A philosophical question is like an inquiry into the constitution of a society. It is as if a society met without clear written rules but in a situation where rules are necessary: the members have an instinct that enables them to observe certain rules in their dealings with one another, but everything is made more difficult because there is no clear pronouncement on the subject, no arrangement for clarifying the rules. Thus they regard one of their number as president, but he does not sit at the head of the table nor is he in any way recognizable and this makes the transaction of business more difficult. So we come along and bring order and clarity. We seat the president at an easily identifiable place with his secretary near him at a special little table, and we seat the other, ordinary members in two rows on either side of the table and so on. . . . (MS 213, 415)

This suggests a certain re-ordering of things by the philosopher, to make everything clear. Not everything in this quotation from the Big Typescript would fit, I think, his view later. But even in *Philosophical Investigations* he says this: "We want to establish an order in our knowledge of the use of language: an order with a particular end in view; one out of many possible orders – not *the* order. . . . the clarity that we are aiming at is indeed *complete* clarity." (*PI*, I, §§132–133) So, it is the task of philosophy to achieve an order, an order which gives complete clarity. This seems much more like some of the traditional, almost imperialistic, views of philosophy than the mere therapeutic view of philosophy as preventing you from banging your head against the limits of language. Wittgenstein is even ready to call philosophy a search for essences: "if we . . . in these investigations are trying to understand the essence of language . . . this means something that already lies open to view and that becomes surveyable by a rearrangement." (*PI*, I, §92) Though this view of philosophy as looking for an order which makes everything surveyable is in some ways like the traditional view of philosophy, Wittgenstein insists that previous philosophy, and especially his own previous philosophy – in *Tractatus Logico-Philosophicus* – went about its search for *Wesen*, for essence, in the wrong way. He makes a contrast between looking at things as a whole to obtain an over-view, and trying to penetrate things to see their metaphysical works, to see what makes them tick, from a metaphysical point of view. He says, describing this mistaken view: "We feel as if we had to *penetrate* phenomena" (*PI*, I, §90), "*The essence is hidden from us*" (*PI*, I, §92); "Something that lies within, which we see when we look *into* the thing, and which an analysis digs out" (*PI*, I, §92).

In particular, Wittgenstein thought, in his earlier philosophy, he had falsely tried to generalize genuine insights. For instance, he had thought that a proposition was a picture. This was a genuine insight, but he had mistakenly tried to make *all* pro-positions of any kind also be pictures. If they did not look like pictures, this must be because we could not see through them; if we could see sufficiently deep inside they really are pictures. That was his view in the *Tractatus*, which now he rejects. He says: "The fatal thing about the scientific way of thinking, which the whole world employs nowadays, is that it wants to produce an explanation in answer to each anxiety."

Of the *Tractatus* he says:

I had used a simile, but because of the grammatical illusion that a concept word has a single thing corresponding to it, the common element in all the objects it applies to, the simile did not seem like one.

Now we have a *theory* . . . but it does not look like a theory. It is typical of such a theory to look at a particular case which is in clear view and say "*That* shows how matters stand in general: this case is the paradigm of every case." "Of course" we say "that's how it has to be" and we have a feeling of satisfaction. We have reached a form of representation which appears *self-evident* to us. But it seems as if we have had a vision of something lying *beneath* the surface. This tendency to generalize the clear case seems to be strictly justified in logic: here we seem to be fully justified in concluding: "If *one* proposition is a picture, then every proposition must be a picture, because they must all share a common essence". For we do indeed suffer from the illusion that the sublime and essential part of our investigation resides in grasping a single all-embracing essence.

That quotation is from the early version of *Philosophical Investigations* which was written before the war (MS 220, 92). It does not appear in the final version of *Philosophical Investigations*. But it is interesting to note his reaction to the picture theory of the *Tractatus* even at this late date. He does not, in effect, say: "It was a total mistake; I was quite wrong to think a proposition was like a picture". He says: "Yes, yes, there is a very clear case in which a proposition is very much like a picture; I was wrong to think that *all* propositions were like this."

Wittgenstein objects to traditional philosophy that it claims to *explain* things, to discover new truths. As early as 1913, in his very earliest surviving work on philosophy, he said that philosophy must only describe, it cannot explain, it must not try to explain. So that it was no new thought in the 1930s that philosophy was not a scientific explanation. But Wittgenstein did come to think that his own *Tractatus* had fallen into the error that it was designed to avoid, that is, of treating philosophy as if it were a kind of science. I quote from *Philosophical Investigations* a passage where he is discussing this *Tractatus* view.

It was true to say that our considerations could not be scientific ones. . . . We may not advance any kind of theory. There must not be anything hypothetical in our considerations. We must do away with all *explanations*, and description alone must take its place. And this description gets its light, that is to say its purpose, from the philosophical problems. These are, of course, not empirical problems; they are solved, rather, by looking into the workings of our language, and that in such a way as to make us recognize those workings: in despite of an urge to misunderstand them. The problems are solved, not by giving new information, but by arranging what we have always known. (*PI*, I, §109)

One feature of all this is important to emphasize in order to reconcile the overview theory of philosophy with the therapeutic theory of philosophy. That is, that Wittgenstein insists that philosophy is only philosophical problems. The survey which you make does not give you the kind of totally new understanding, a surplus understanding, it merely removes the philosophical problems. Philosophy is not anything over and above the problems and their removal. The clearest statements of this are in *Philosophical Grammar*, but they are echoed later. Wittgenstein says in *Philosophical Grammar*:

Philosophy isn't anything except philosophical problems, the particular individual worries that we call "philosophical problems". Their common element extends as far as the common element in different regions of our language. (*PG*, p. 193)

"Philosophy", like so many other words, is a family-likeness word: there is no one thing in common to everything that is philosophy. In the same context, having said that '*Sprache*' — language — is a family-likeness concept, so that there is no single essence of language, he goes on to say:

If the general concept of language dissolves in this way, doesn't philosophy dissolve as well? No, for the task of philosophy is not to create a new, ideal language, but to clarify the use of our language. . . . its aim is to remove particular misunderstandings;

not to produce a real understanding for the first time. (*PG*, p. 115)

There is one philosophical remark to which Wittgenstein attached great importance: he wrote it very early on, it is in the Big Typescript and earlier, and it appears also in *Philosophical Investigations*, but he continued to reconsider it after *Philosophical Investigations* was all ready for the press. It is the following remark:

> The real discovery is the one that makes me capable of stopping doing philosophy when I want to – the one that gives philosophy peace, so that it is no longer tormented by questions which bring *itself* in question. – Instead, we now demonstrate a method, by examples; and the series of examples can be broken off. – Problems are solved (difficulties eliminated), not a *single* problem. . . . "But then we will never come to the end of our job!" Of course not, because it has no end. (MS 213, 431f.)

Now, why did Wittgenstein say that the important discovery was the one that let him stop doing philosophy whenever he wanted? It seems a very strange thing to say. It would be absurd to say, for instance, that the most important musical discovery is the one which enables you to stop making music when you want. Why should he say the important discovery in philosophy is one that enables you to stop philosophizing?

What Wittgenstein is attacking there is the view that philosophy is something that you have to do before you can do anything else; the view that until philosophy has been gotten over with nothing else is reliable; the view that philosophy is a *foundation* of things. Such a view was held very explicitly by Descartes. Descartes said that knowledge was a tree of which metaphysics – by which he meant largely epistemology – was the root, with physics as the trunk and various branches such as medicine, mechanics, and morals. What Wittgenstein is attacking is the idea that the whole tree will not grow unless you have the roots, the metaphor implicit in the description of philosophical studies as being foundational studies. Clearly, if you have the foundational view of philosophy you cannot stop philosophizing whenever you want to; until you get these roots dug in, until you get the foundations built, you cannot do anything else, so it would be irresponsible for the philosopher to stop. The real discovery, then, is the one that you can stop when you want to – you are not going to spoil anything else.

There are many passages in Wittgenstein which attack the idea that philosophy provides a foundation. For instance:

> Philosophy solves, or rather gets rid of, only philosophical problems; it does not set our thinking on a more solid basis. What I am attacking is above all the idea that the question "what is knowledge" – e.g. – is a crucial one. That is what it seems to be: it seems as if we didn't yet know anything at all until we can answer *that* question. In our philosophical investigations it is as if we were in a terrible hurry to complete a backlog of unfinished business which has to be finished or else everything else seems to hang in the air. (MS 219, 10)

In fact it is quite absurd to say: "We cannot know anything at all until we know what knowing is." To use an example Wittgenstein often uses, that is as foolish as to say: "We cannot spell any words at all, unless we can spell 'spelling'." There is no metamathematics, Wittgenstein says, philosophy is not meta-anything; that is, it is not a science which studies a discipline as a whole and gives it a foundation. It is not a second-order activity at all. "One might think: if philosophy speaks of the use of the word 'philosophy' there must be a second-order philosophy" (*PI*, I, §121). "The philosophy of logic speaks of sentences and words in exactly the same sense in which we speak of them in ordinary life . . ." (*PI*, I, §108). Orthography is not a second-order science: you spell the word 'spelling' the same way as you spell any other word.

Now I come to my main question. If the value of philosophy is simply that it gets rid of philosophical worries, and that it solves philosophical problems, then why do philosophy at all? Is there not a simpler way of getting rid of these worries and these problems, namely, never look at a book of philosophy! Do not get as far as the problems and then you will not need the answers! Thus you would be saved a lot of anguish and society would be saved a lot of money. If philosophy is only good against philosophers, why do philosophy at all?

At best, philosophy might be like germ warfare. Several countries have establishments for inventing the most terrible weapons of germ warfare. If you meet people who work in these establishments you naturally wonder at them and ask: "Why do you work at this kind of job – inventing new diseases to give to human beings?" They always give you the answer: "We need to know what it may be that our enemies are planning. Unless we try and invent things for use against others we will not know what terrible things *they* are going to do to us. We do not really intend to give these diseases to everybody else, we just want to know how to deal with them if other people use such weapons against us." On this account of Wittgenstein's view of philosophy it seems as if philosophers are people like those who work in a germ warfare department. It is perhaps justifiable to work on these strange cultures that are going to produce the most extraordinary intellectual diseases, but it is justifiable only on the count that there are already other people who are producing these horrible things and you have to produce them yourself to know how to deal with them.

Not liking the comparison between philosophy and germ warfare I want to look at what Wittgenstein says to see if there is perhaps another way that one can interpret it. "What is the use of philosophy if it is only useful against other philosophers?" is a question that was put with characteristic vigour by Professor Gilbert Ryle. You remember one of Wittgenstein's most famous descriptions of the purpose of philosophy is given in

Philosophical Investigations: "What is your aim in philosophy? – To show the fly the way out of the fly-bottle" (*PI*, I, §309). Ryle asked: "What has a fly lost, who never got into a fly-bottle?"

In an unpublished manuscript there is a very clear answer to the question "Why do philosophy, if it is only useful against philosophers?" Wittgenstein says: "Philosophy is a tool which is useful only against philosophers and against the philosopher in us" (MS 219, 11). It is only useful against philosophers, yes, but also against *the philosopher in us*. Wittgenstein's answer to the question "Why do philosophy at all, if it is only useful against philosophical errors?" is that every one of us, every human being, is trapped in philosophical errors. And there are a number of indications that suggest Wittgenstein believed philosophy to be an unavoidable part of the human condition. He quotes with approval, for instance, the remark of Lichtenberg: "Our whole philosophy is the rectification of linguistic usage: the rectification, that is, of a philosophy which is the most universal philosophy." I think Wittgenstein endorsed the idea. In the Big Typescript he says: "Philosophy is embodied not in propositions, but in a language" (MS 213, 425). The philosophy which is embedded in our language is a bad philosophy – it is a mythology. Wittgenstein says. "In our language there is an entire mythology embodied" (MS 213, 434). He gives an instance of what he means: "The primitive forms of our language – noun, adjective, and verb – show the simple picture to which it tries to make everything conform."

When Wittgenstein says that there is a mythology in our language, this is not a total condemnation (Wittgenstein's attitude to myths was a many-sided one), but it is not a justification either. Some myths, certainly, are something to be got rid of; and if some are to be retained, we must recognize them as myths. The question then is in what way – according to Wittgenstein – is the philosopher better off than an ordinary non-philosopher? Is there any way in which he is better off? The answer, I think, is yes. This does not mean that it is to everybody's advantage to become a philosopher; but if you do philosophy in the right spirit, then you are better off than somebody who has done no philosophy. It is not because you know more that you are better off: you do not know anything that anybody else does not know, and one of the temptations of philosophy, which makes it a dangerous thing to take up, is that you may get the impression that you do know more than other people. But still, you are better off, if you have done philosophy in the right way: not because you know more, but because you have gone through a discipline which enables you to resist certain temptations.

This comes out in a remark of Wittgenstein's about Tolstoy. In "What is Art?" Tolstoy makes it the criterion of value for a work of art that it should be intelligible to everybody; that is why certain short stories and the Bible are magnificent art but why the operas of the nineteenth-century composers are totally worthless. I quote from the Big Typescript:

> Tolstoy: "The significance of an object lies in its universal intelligibility". That is partly true, partly false. When an object is significant and important what makes it difficult to understand is not the lack of some special instruction in abstruse matters necessary for its understanding, but the conflict between the right understanding of the object and what most men *want* to see. This can make the most obvious things the most difficult to understand. What has to be overcome is not a difficulty of the understanding, but of the will. (MS 213, 406–7)

And he says that in philosophy as in architecture: "The job to be done is . . . really a job on oneself" (*ibid.*).

Wittgenstein thinks that the task of philosophy is not to enlighten the intellect, or not directly, but to work upon the will, to strengthen one to resist certain temptations. Wittgenstein's account of why we have to philosophize, or why it is worthwhile to philosophize even though philosophy is only useful against philosophical problems, is rather like the Christian doctrine of original sin. According to the Christian doctrine we are all born in a state of sin; according to Wittgenstein we are not born in the state of philosophical sin, but we take it in along with language. Along with language, along with all the benefits which language brings, along with all the possibilities for our way of life which it brings, we take in whether we want to or not, certain temptations; we must resist these if we are not to be misled. There are several passages where Wittgenstein speaks of the temptation or bewitchment of language. One very well-known one from *Philosophical Investigations* concerns the philosophy of mathematics and the inclination we have to say certain things about mathematics.

> What we 'are tempted to say' in such a case, is, of course, not philosophy – but its raw material. Thus, for example, what a mathematician is inclined to say about the objectivity and reality of mathematical facts, is not a philosophy of mathematics, but something for philosophical *treatment*. (*PI*, I, §254)

In the Big Typescript Wittgenstein gives a lively illustration of the temptations. He says:

> Learning philosophy has the same kind of extraordinary difficulty that geography lessons would have if the pupils began with a lot of false and oversimplified ideas about the way rivers and mountain ranges go. (MS 213, 423)

It is as with the maps which the railways, for example, the London Underground, provide, which simplify the way in which the railways go; they make it look as if they go in rectangular tracks. Wittgenstein is suggesting that we come to learn the philosophy of language with a sort of preconception as if a child coming to a geography lesson believed that the railway maps showed the shape in which the world was, that the rivers and mountains were all square, etc.

Human beings are profoundly enmeshed in philosophical – i.e. grammatical – confusions. They cannot be freed without first being extricated from the extraordinary variety of associations which hold them prisoner. You have as it were to reconstitute their entire language. – But this language grew up as it did because human beings had – and have – the tendency to think in this way. So you can only succeed in extricating people who live in an instinctive rebellion against language; you cannot help those whose entire instinct is to live in the herd which has created this language as its own proper mode of expression. (MS 213, 423)

This, to my ear, resembles the type of language of St Augustine. Augustine thought that we were all a "*massa damnata*": by being born into this race we were born into a damned race, and only those who were not at home in the world, those who found that they had to push against it, really had a hope of salvation. The comparison between philosophy and conversion, philosophy and renunciation of the world, is very explicit in the Big Typescript. Just as Augustine would think that in renouncing the world, the flesh, and the devil one is not giving up anything that is really worthwhile, so Wittgenstein says about philosophy:

> As I have often said, philosophy does not call on me for any sacrifice, because I am not denying myself the saying of anything but simply giving up certain combinations of words as senseless. But in another sense philosophy demands a renunciation, but a renunciation of feeling, not of understanding. Perhaps that is what makes it so hard for many people. It can be as hard to refrain from using an expression as it is to hold back tears or hold in anger. (MS 213, 406)

Up to this point then, the answer to the question "Why go into philosophy?" is that we are all philosophers, bad or good, whether we choose it or not; we are made philosophers by our language. But that is not the full answer to the question, because Wittgenstein also often says that philosophical errors or problems do not trouble us in practical life. The title of a whole section of the Big Typescript goes like this:

It is not in practical life that we encounter philosophical problems (as we may encounter scientific problems) — it is when we start constructing sentences not for practical purposes but under the influence of certain analogies in language. (MS 213, 427)

And in several places he says that Augustine's question "What is time?" is not the kind of thing that really bothers people when they are using their watches or keeping appointments.

Someone who is engaged in measuring time will not be bothered by this problem. He will *use* language and not notice the problem at all. In his hand, we might say, language is soft and pliable; in the hands of others — philosophers — it suddenly becomes hard and stiff and begins to display difficulties. Philosophers as it were freeze language and make it rigid. (MS 219, 24)

It is when language is idling, etc., that these difficulties come. Why then do philosophy if philosophical confusion does no practical harm? I conjecture that Wittgenstein would answer as follows. An ordinary person, a simple human being who takes no interest in philosophy, has as a user of language, a temptation to all kinds of philosophical misunderstandings. If he is lucky these will not harm him at all; certainly they will not harm him when he is going about his daily business. However, he is liable to suffer in two ways.

First of all, the plain man is vulnerable to the persuasions of the bad philosophers and the bad scientists. Let us suppose he is a victim of the mythology of the mental process, the belief that all kinds of strange mental processes go on in cases where experience reveals no such process, but our language suggests that one must occur. Such a person is not impeded in his communication with other people in the ordinary way by these theories, but on the other hand, he may come across a psychologist who has built a theory on them and on its basis erected doctrines about how children shall be taught in school. Without philosophy you are defenceless against that sort of pseudo-scientific persuasion.

Secondly, not only is the plain man vulnerable in that way, but he is weak in another way. He is unqualified to go in for any scientific inquiry, because once he investigates anything scientifically, the philosophical errors will then begin to matter. In terms of the medical analogy, he is like somebody with a weak heart, who, if he lives a quiet life, and if there are no epidemics, may well live as long and as peaceful a life as everybody else, but because his heart is weak he may be one of the first people who suffer when an epidemic comes in and who will not be good for any expedition which involves climbing mountains or going into difficult climates. The non-philosophical person, if he takes up a science, is like a man with a weak heart who tries to climb Mount Everest; the philosophical errors from ordinary language that have not impeded him in milking his cows or sewing his shirt, begin really to matter.

Even before that, in addition to being vulnerable to pseudo-scientists the plain man is vulnerable to bad mythology. Wittgenstein, despite his sympathetic attitude to mythology, thought that there could be very bad mythologies: he felt, for instance, that the doctrine of the scapegoat was a bad mythology. The idea that you could get rid of your guilt and put it onto an animal, understood simply as mythology, is a bad, a degrading, thing to believe. This is an instance of the kind of thing which the plain man without philosophy is vulnerable to. If he then takes a step further and tries to turn his bad mythology into a theology, if he makes it scientific study, then of course it is worse. In the Big Typescript Wittgenstein says that crude ideas of the soul are less dangerous than sophisticated ones:

As long as you imagine the soul as a *thing*, a *body* in the head, this hypothesis is not at all dangerous. It is not the crudity and incompleteness of our models that brings danger, but their vagueness.

The danger begins when we notice that the old model is inadequate and then instead of altering it as it were sublimate it. As long as I say that thought is in my head, there is nothing wrong; things become dangerous when we say that thought is not in my head but in my spirit. (MS 213, 434–435)

There are then, three areas of danger for someone undisciplined by philosophy: at the mythical level, at the hypermythical or theological level, and at the scientific level.

Wittgenstein's views on the relationship between science and philosophy are difficult to understand. On the one hand, he seems to say that philosophy leaves all the other sciences just as they are, has nothing to say to them, does not alter them or give them foundations. At the same time, he seems to say that unless you are a philosopher you are going to make the most terrible scientific mistakes. He says this especially in connection with the two sciences whose philosophy he was most interested in: psychology and mathematics. There is a familiar passage in *Philosophical Investigations*:

Philosophy may in no way interfere with the actual use of language — it can in the end only describe it.
For it cannot give it any foundation either.
It leaves everything as it is.
It also leaves mathematics as it is, and no mathematical discovery can advance it. (*PI*, I, §124)

It is, I think, misleading to say that philosophy leaves mathematics exactly as it is. In the sense in which Wittgenstein means it, it is correct; but the obvious way to read that passage is that mathematics and philosophy are independent of each other and progress in one cannot affect progress in the other, a mistake in one cannot affect a mistake in the other. That is not what he means, as you only have to set beside this text a rather comic passage about mathematics and philosophy in *Philosophical Grammar* in order to see.

> Philosophical clarity will have the same effect on the growth of mathematics as sunlight has on the growth of potato shoots. (In a dark cellar they grow yards long.) (*PG*, p. 381)

If it is true that mathematics will grow to a gigantic length if it is left in its dark cellar, but in the daylight of philosophy will only grow so big, then how can we say that philosophy leaves mathematics just as it is? In fact there are numerous passages which show that Wittgenstein thought that philosophy does affect other disciplines in practice, especially mathematics and psychology. For instance he says that it is simple philosophical mistakes that mathematicians make which lead them to make very complicated mistakes in mathematics.

> If a philosopher draws the attention of a mathematician to a distinction, or a misleading mode of expression, the mathematician always says 'Sure, we know all that, it isn't really very interesting.' He does not realise that when he is troubled by philosophical questions it is because of those very unclarities that he passed over earlier with a shrug of the shoulders. (MS 219, 10)

And again from *Philosophical Grammar*:

> A philosopher feels changes in the style of a derivation which a contemporary mathematician passes over calmly with a blank face. What will distinguish the mathematician of the future from those of today will really be a greater sensitivity, and *that* will – as it were – prune mathematics; since people will then be more intent on absolute clarity than on the discovery of new games. (*PG*, p. 381)

The solution to this apparent inconsistency about the relationship between philosophy and mathematics is this: that mathematics as a discipline is not responsible to philosophy; but the people who are mathematicians are human beings who suffer from the original sin of using the philosophically misleading language. It is not while they are doing mathematics but while they are talking ordinary language about mathematics that they reveal their philosophical mistakes. This may, human nature being what it is, lead them also to make mistakes or useless moves in their mathematics.

Wittgenstein says, strikingly, that the philosopher is not a citizen of any human community, and that is what makes him a philosopher. And he contrasts the good philosopher, who stands outside the human communities, with bourgeois philosophers of whom he gives Frank Ramsey as an example. He regarded Ramsey as a bourgeois philosopher because he was willing to take mathematics more or less as it stood and just as the mathematicians of his age described it. According to Wittgenstein he was a sort of propagandist for the current regime in mathematics. The real philosopher must stand outside. Of course, he stands outside mathematics because he is a philosopher and not a mathematician; but Wittgenstein means something more than that: he must distance himself from the mathematical community, that is, the community of those who use our human language with the temptations that it brings. And in *Philosophical Investigations* he thinks and says the same things about the psychologists. Psychology is barren, he says, because of conceptual confusions. I think that what he has there in mind is experimental psychologists who start from a mythological view of the nature of mental processes, which they take from ordinary language, and accept unquestioned, as if it were the experimental basis of their research.

So much for Wittgenstein's view of the relation between philosophy and the common sense of the ordinary man, and between philosophy and other disciplines. I want to end by discussing something about which I feel rather uncertain: how did Wittgenstein think philosophy as *he* did it and as *he* conceived it was related to traditional philosophy? It is clear that he thought at least sometimes that he was doing philosophy in a very different way from the great philosophers, the traditional philosophers. He often uses 'philosophers' almost as a term of abuse, as a term of criticism. For instance:

> When philosophers use a word . . . and try to grasp the *essence* of the thing, one must always ask oneself: is the word ever actually used in this way in the language-game that is its original home? – What *we* do is to bring words back from their metaphysical to their everyday use. (*PI*, I, §116)

Sometimes Wittgenstein says fairly contemptuous things about philosophers, for instance that "philosophers are often like little children who scribble a jumble of lines on a piece of paper and then ask grown-ups 'what is that?'" (MS 213, 430).

He has a consciousness of a big difference between himself and other philosophers. He says:

> A common-sense person, when he reads earlier philosophers thinks – quite rightly – "Sheer nonsense". When he listens to me, he thinks – rightly again – "Nothing but stale truisms". That is how the image of philosophy has changed. (MS 219, 6)

I want to end by putting the question: *was* there such a big difference between Wittgenstein's philosophy and traditional philosophy as he thought?

Wittgenstein himself raises a very interesting question: Is there any progress in philosophy? Some people find philosophy the most attractive of all the disciplines for the following reason: philosophy seems on the one hand to be like a science in that one is in pursuit of truth; there seem to be truths which are discovered in philosophy, certain things which we understand which even the greatest philosophers of previous generations did not understand. So, as a philosopher, one has the excitement of belonging to an ongoing cooperative cumulative process in the way that a scientist does, and one has therefore the hope that one may make one's tiny contribution to the building of the great edifice. Thus philosophy has one of the attractions of science. On the other hand, philosophy seems to have the attraction of the arts, of the humanistic disciplines, in that classic works of philosophy do not date. If we want to learn physics or chemistry, as opposed to their history, we do not nowadays read Newton or Faraday. Whereas in literature, we read Homer and Shakespeare not merely in order to know the quaint things that people used to think in those far-off days. So philosophy seems attractive in that it combines being a discipline in pursuit of truth in which things are discovered as in a science, with being a humane discipline in which a great work does not age, as in literature.

Wittgenstein would surely not have approved of what I have just said, but he did put himself the question how far is there progress in philosophy. He says:

> You always hear people say that philosophy makes no progress and that the same philosophical problems which were already preoccupying the Greeks are still troubling us today. But people who say that do not understand the reason why it has to be so. The reason is that our language has remained the same and always introduces us to the same questions. As long as there is a verb "be" which seems to work like "eat" and "drink"; as long as there are adjectives like "identical" "true" "false" "possible"; as long as people speak of the passage of time and of the extent of space, and so on; as long as all this happens people will always run up against the same teasing difficulties and will stare at something which no explanation seems able to remove. . . . I read ". . . philosophers are no nearer to the meaning of 'reality' than Plato

got. . . ." What an extraordinary thing! How remarkable that
Plato could get so far! Or that we have not been able to get any
further! Was it because Plato was *so* clever? (MS 213, 424)

Wittgenstein does not give as ample an answer to the question
as his philosophical views as I have described them would allow
him to. Even given the comparatively narrow view of
philosophy which he argued for, there are various ways in
which philosophy can progress. One way in which you could
say that there is progress in philosophy, but perhaps not a very
comforting one, is the way in which there is progress in the
expansion of π. That is to say, mathematicians have made great
progress since the days of Pythagoras in the expansion of π; they
can expand it to many, many more places than anybody could
in ancient Greece. None the less, in another sense, there is no
progress, they are no nearer to the end of the expansion of π
than Pythagoras was. But there is more to progress in
philosophy than that.

Suppose we take first the therapeutic, pessimistic view of
philosophy. On this view there is room for progress in
philosophy in one of the ways in which there is room for
progress in medicine, that is, that as the human race continues
and grows older new diseases which were never before heard
of, need cures. Philosophical therapy must cure the
philosophical diseases from which we suffer, but from which
earlier generations were free. But if you take the more op-
timistic aspect of philosophy as a search for *Übersichtlichkeit* −
knowing one's way around, to use another of Wittgenstein's
metaphors − philosophy is like a guide to the city, a guide to the
workings of language, thought of as a city. The city of
languages, as Wittgenstein says, has many different parts: there
is the *Altstadt* with the old buildings, cramped together and not
much room but very interesting and exciting, and then there are
the great new buildings outside, the sciences, ordered and

regimented. As there are new suburbs, so there are new places for the philosopher to guide one around.

But for Wittgenstein there is one very important sense in which there could not be progress in philosophy. This is because philosophy is a matter of the will, not of the intellect. Philosophy is something which everybody must do for himself; an activity which is essentially, not just accidentally, a striving against one's own intellectual temptations. It is clear that this cannot be something which is so done once for all by the human race in the seventeenth-century and then does not need to be done again. It is characteristic of scientific research that if the research is well done, it does not need to be done again. If you have to repeat a piece of scientific research it shows that either the research was botched to begin with or that other things have happened since which place it in a different context. In the case of curing an individual sickness or in the case of mental discipline one cannot say that once done it need not be done again. It must be done for each person afresh: in that way everybody has to start again and there is no progress. This insight of Wittgenstein's seems to me correct; but I do not think it means in any way that his thought is as discontinuous with the great tradition of Western philosophy as he sometimes seems to have believed it was. Of course Wittgenstein was hostile to metaphysics, to the pretensions of rationalistic philosophy to prove the existence of God, the immortality of the soul, to go far beyond the bounds of experience. He was hostile to that; but then so was Immanuel Kant. Wittgenstein was against the search for essences, for a unique essence common to all uses of the word, but so, after all were the medieval scholastics who developed the theory of analogy. Wittgenstein was insistent that all our intellectual inquiries depend for the possibility of their existence on all kinds of simple, natural, inexplicable, original impulses of human mind; but so, for very similar reasons, was David Hume. Wittgenstein was anxious that the philosopher should distinguish between parts of speech, which the grammarians lump together; where the grammarians for instance talk about verbs the philosopher must distinguish within this overbroad category between processes and conditions and dispositions, etc. But almost word for word the distinctions made in this spirit in the "Brown Book" and elsewhere correspond to the distinctions between the different types of *hexeis* and the different types of *energeia* in Aristotle.

Finally, Wittgenstein's insistence that philosophy is something that each man must do for himself, and which is a matter of the will, not of the intellect, resembles most of all the philosopher with whom he is most frequently contrasted, René Descartes. Descartes's philosophical masterpiece was not a textbook but a series of meditations which each person must go through for himself; the doubt and the *cogito* was a discipline which each person must administer to himself. Descartes embraced the idea that the philosophy was a matter of the will, not of the intellect, so enthusiastically that he said that judgement itself was an act of the will.

In philosophy of mind, the importance of Wittgenstein in history arises from his exposure of confusion which philosophy inherited from Descartes. But in the matter of the nature of philosophy Descartes and Wittgenstein are fundamentally at one.

Freud and Wittgenstein

Brian McGuinness

Wittgenstein's remarks about Freud amount to no systematic or reasoned criticism of psychoanalysis. Their origin alone explains this. They occur in the course of notes made by Rhees on conversations, or else are scattered through Wittgenstein's own notebooks at points where he was talking about some general topic – symbolism or myth or science – which also has connections with Freud. (The latter, now printed in *Culture and Value* (1980), are more fully authentic and more strikingly expressed and I draw slightly more on them, but readers of *Lectures and Conversations on Aesthetics* (1966) will not find the picture essentially changed.)

Wittgenstein told Rhees that he first read Freud sometime after 1919. In 1940 he still regarded himself as a disciple or follower of Freud, a claim that has been found surprising, but which I hope to make more plausible. His reading seems to have been in the interpretative works from before World War I: he quotes the *Psychopathology of Everyday Life* and (above all) the *Interpretation of Dreams*. But he will have known a good deal more simply by osmosis. A small example is that *Studies in Hysteria* was to be found in the libraries of his family and he seems to have formed some idea as to its contents, as appears from the following entry in a 1939 notebook:

I believe that my originality (if that is the right word) is an originality belonging to the soil rather than to the seed. (Perhaps I have no seed of my own.) Sow a seed in my soil and it will grow differently than it would in any other soil.

Freud's originality too was like this, I think. I have always believed – without knowing why – that the real germ of psychoanalysis came from Breuer, not Freud. Of course Breuer's seedgrain can only have been quite tiny. ['may have been quite minute' is also a possible translation and, I think, more probable. B.McG.] (*Culture and Value*, p. 36; passage dated 1939–40)

As is well known, Freud freely acknowledged that much of his work consisted in a development of "the great discoveries" of Breuer: particularly was this true of the view of psychoanalysis as an interpretative art, which was the aspect that most interested Wittgenstein. Earlier in the 1930s Wittgenstein had already used the relation of Freud to Breuer as a parallel for his own situation: he thought it was characteristic of a Jewish thinker to be merely reproductive; his own task has been not to discover a new way of thinking but to clarify those given him by others. He then wonders whether it is right to say that Freud was inspired by Breuer, just as he, Wittgenstein, was inspired by Boltzmann, Hertz, Schopenhauer, Frege, Russell, Kraus, Loos, Weininger, Spengler, Sraffa. (It will be noted that some of those who inspired Wittgenstein were, like Breuer, Jews.) I believe (though this can only be speculation) that Breuer interested Wittgenstein because Breuer himself renounced the pursuit or exploration of the insights won together with Freud. There were dangers in this new art. Wittgenstein points to those dangers in his conversations with Rhees and also in another remark of 1939–40:

In a way having oneself psychoanalysed is like eating from the tree of knowledge. The knowledge acquired sets us (new) ethical problems; but contributes nothing to their solution. (*Culture and Value*, p. 34)

Wittgenstein was indeed acquainted with the practice of analysis: he had lived, it is enough to say, through the 1920s in or

near Vienna. Friends and relations had looked to it as a way out
of their personal problems: Wittgenstein was inclined to think
that the chief good it would do them would reside in the shame
they were bound to feel at all the things they would have to
reveal to their analyst. He himself had to undergo a psychological examination for legal reasons: we know nothing of
its outcome or his reaction, except the resentment he felt at the
loss of privacy, always characteristic of him and likely to be in-
creased by the compulsory nature of this examination. His sister,
on the other hand, was analysed by Freud and largely from
speculative curiosity. She and Wittgenstein would exchange
dream reports and give interpretations of each other's dreams. It
was a kind of playing with the mind that they both found
attractive. In a somewhat similar spirit they both had themselves
hypnotized – at widely remote times and for different purposes.
Wittgenstein's purpose was to see whether hypnosis, which
made man capable of lifting great weights, would make him
capable of the superhuman efforts of concentration needed to
solve the problems of the foundations of mathematics. As for
hypnosis, both brother and sister proved impossible to hyp-
notize during the session but fell into a deep trance the moment
it was over. How common such counter-suggestibility is I do
not know. The fascination with dreams and the freedom of interpretation assumed are important for understanding
Wittgenstein's attitude towards Freud. More even than a work
of art, a piece of music, or a work of literature, a dream seemed
to call out for interpretation. Its meaning was not there all at
once but would appear only in the course of further discussion.
The understanding of a dream was a particularly good example
of the truth that the understanding of anything might well be a
process extended in time; thus even in speech and even in
philosophy you may discover what I mean before I do. This
theme was to appear often in Wittgenstein's philosophy.
Another that he often dwelt on and which was well illustrated
by the interpretation of dreams (and the Freudian method in

particular) was the complicated way in which the human mind
made pictures of facts – in this case so complicated that the
picture given hardly deserves the name, as he says in a
manuscript of 1944 (*Culture and Value*, p. 44).

This sketch of the background of Wittgenstein's interest in
Freud will help, I hope, to prepare us for the main point in
Freud that gets discussed: namely the criteria of dream interpretation. Freud was, Wittgenstein thought, very clever at interpretation: '*geistreich*' – the word contains a hint of criticism,
and it is a fairly common criticism of himself by Wittgenstein
that he was too attached to this quality. Freud then was clever
enough to produce interpretations which, in part because of
their ingenuity, were attractive. Did Wittgenstein want us to
regard them as embodying pseudo-explanations? Not exactly,
as I think can best be shown by considering the following
passage:

> In a Freudian analysis the dream is, so to speak, decomposed. It
> completely loses its original meaning. One could imagine the
> dream as something performed on the stage, whose action was
> sometimes rather incomprehensible but in part quite comprehen-
> sible, at least in our eyes: now, one might imagine, the action of
> the play is torn into small parts and each part is given a quite new
> meaning. Or one could imagine a large piece of paper with a
> picture drawn on it: the picture is now pleated up in such a way
> that pieces which were quite unrelated in the original picture are
> now visually adjacent and a new picture (meaningful or
> meaningless) results: this new picture would be the dream as
> dreamed, while the original picture would correspond to the
> latent dream content.
>
>   Now, I could imagine someone who saw the unfolded picture
> exclaiming, "Yes, that is the solution, that is what I dreamt, but
> without the gaps and distortions". In that case the solution would
> be constituted as such by the dreamer's recognition of it and by
> nothing else. It is just as when you are writing something and
> looking for a word and suddenly say "*That*'s it, *that*'s what I
> wanted to say": your recognition of the word stamps it as the

word that you were looking for and have now found. (Here is a case where you really could say, rather in the way Russell speaks about wishing, that you only know what you have been looking for when you have found it.)

What is intriguing about a dream is not its causal connection with events in my life etc. but rather that it functions as part (indeed a very lifelike part) of a story the remainder of which is in the dark. (One wants to ask, "Where did this figure suddenly come from, and what happened to it?") Indeed, even when someone subsequently shows me that the original story wasn't a proper story at all but was really based on a quite different story, so that I am inclined to exclaim, in disillusion, "Oh, is that what it was!", even then the impression remains that I have been robbed of something. To be sure, as the paper unfolds the original picture disintegrates – the man that I saw was taken from *there*, his words from *here*, the surroundings of the dream from a third place, but the dream-story has its peculiar charm, like a painting that attracts and inspires us.

Of course one might say that we *view* the dream in an inspired way, it is we that are inspired. Because when we relate our dream to someone else, generally the imagery doesn't inspire him. The dream affects us like an idea pregnant with possible developments. (*Culture and Value*, pp. 68–9; passage dated 1948; my own translation.)

Wittgenstein's fondness for analogies will be seen from the passsage. It was in the invention of analogies that he thought he came nearest to originality, according to the passages on originality that I have partly quoted. Some of his analogies – pictures, games, etc. – have proved useful tools for thinking. But the analogy of the pleated paper in this case is one that Wittgenstein means us to view with suspicion. Sometimes we feel like saying "So that's what it was!" but it is only our now feeling that that makes it (if the word is appropriate) true. Wittgenstein is suggesting that there is not really a full and coherent picture or story there all the time. What is there at the earlier stage is an idea capable of development. The latent content is created by the development, which might have taken a quite other course with equal validity, for it is evident what answer to the question about the criteria for the interpretation of dreams is implicit in our passage. Acknowledgement, acceptance, or recognition is the sort of criterion envisaged. I say *the sort of* criterion because (as the conversations with Rhees make clear) Wittgenstein thinks Freud sometimes talks as if the right interpretation might be clearer to the doctor than to the patient, or as if the right interpretation were the one whose acceptance by the patient would lead to the most favourable outcome to treatment. Much thought has been devoted to this matter and I will not pronounce on it here, though it seems plausible to say with Wittgenstein that in practice a blend of these criteria is employed. What is important for the question about criteria is not how exactly these things are worked out in the therapeutic situation, but that they are worked out there. The right interpretation is one that works, that is to say one that contributes most to the activity being jointly conducted by the doctor and patient. Generally that will mean one which the dreamer either embraces or rejects, not one to which he is indifferent. The correct interpretation – or rather, as we must say, a correct interpretation – will be one that says something to the patient.

This brings us to the other theme of the passage quoted from Wittgenstein. In any such interpretation there is something lost, namely and precisely the richness and indeterminate character of the original dream. The dreamer must be prepared to sacrifice this if he is to take part in the joint activity with the analyst already mentioned. Not only must he be prepared to accept interpretations of his dream, but also to accept as correct only those interpretations that relate his dream to figures and wishes from his past. In doing so he is (in Wittgenstein's terms) accepting a mythology propounded by Freud. Wittgenstein gave one or two examples in his conversations with Rhees to show the attractiveness of this mythology:

The attractiveness of the suggestion, for instance, that all anxiety is a repetition of the anxiety of the birth trauma, is just the attractiveness of a mythology. "It is all the outcome of something that happened long ago." Almost like referring to a totem.

Much the same could be said of the notion of an "Urszene". This often has the attractiveness of giving a sort of tragic pattern to one's life. It is all the repetition of the same pattern which was settled long ago. Like a tragic figure carrying out the decrees under which the fates had placed him at birth. Many people have at some period, serious trouble in their lives – so serious as to lead to thoughts of suicide. This is likely to appear to one as something nasty, as a situation which is too foul to be a subject of a tragedy. And it may then be an immense relief if it can be shown that one's life has the pattern rather of a tragedy – the tragic working-out and repetition of a pattern which was determined by the primal scene. (*Lectures and Conversations* (1966), p. 51)

We shall see that it is by no means a condemnation of Freud's thought to call it a mythology. A myth to function as such must say something to human beings, and Freud's is a powerful mythology. What the mythological character of the thought does rule out is its forming a science. The test of a science used by Wittgenstein is its dependence on experiment to establish causal laws, and he points to the absence of experimental evidence in psychoanalytical explanations. He does not spend long on this point, discussions of which I can assume to be familiar to readers. Therapeutic success, if it can be identified, is not experimental evidence of the required kind. It establishes only that the result of the therapy is acceptable to society or to the patient – it testifies only to, it consists in, the effectiveness or the welcome nature of the mythology, of the stories told. It has itself nothing to do with their truth. There can of course be small areas in which an apparently scientific method can be applied – if for example (and it is an example given by Wittgenstein) one formed the hypothesis on the basis of dream

reports that the dreamer can be brought to recall such and such
memories. This hypothesis might or might not be verified.
What would success in such prediction show? Primarily the
effectiveness of the technique in leading from one avowal to
another; but even if the memories so reached were always
veridical, there would be no proof of the psychodynamic ap-
paratus invoked to account for the route from the original event
to the dream report. We should just have the fact that a certain
dream report (or set of dream reports) could be read as the
expression of certain memories, without any means of
explaining how this came about. If a great degree of success
with all sorts of subjects were achieved in respect of dream and
memories, the result would be very striking, though, I think, no
more a justification for a causal hypothesis than a similar
hypothetical success in astrology. In practice, however, success
of this kind is achieved only with patients already thinking in
ways favourable to the analytic process. In their case a communication conveyed in the oblique way typical of that process
bears witness only to the whole-heartedness of their participa-
tion in it. They have enabled the analyst to understand them
before they understood themselves.

The contrast between a psychoanalytic explanation and a
scientific one can be made clearer by taking an example not
actually used by Wittgenstein – that of slips or errors in the
transmission of texts. Here there has grown up in the course of
centuries of critical work on transmission a modest science
which embodies the most frequent forms of corruption in a set
of principles. There is for instance the error of trivialization –
the familiar word is substituted for the unusual but correct one;
or *le saut du même au même* – the eye of the copyist (or his
memory when he recites to himself a passage he is in the course
of copying) jumps either forward or back from one occurrence
of a word or word-element to another, thus resulting either in
an omission or a repetition. Countless instances of these errors

can be found, and most slips discussed by Freud in the *Psychopathology of Everyday Life* can be explained on such principles without great difficulty. This has been shown by Sebastiano Timpanaro in his book *The Freudian Slip* (London, 1976), on which I draw heavily. (It would also be possible, no doubt, to embody such principles in a study of attention in general by the methods of experimental psychology, but in practice the empirical evidence available in the special field of the transmission of texts, together with some fairly elementary common-sense reflections, suffices.)

What good then does Freud's account of the origin of these slips (as they occur, say, in memories or quotations) do? It attempts to show why just these errors (and not all the others that would also be possible according to the principles) occurred. But we are not entitled to suppose that there has to be a reason why just these errors occurred, just as we cannot demand a cause for every coincidence. The scribe's liability to certain types of error is activated in a particular case by the state of the weather, the fact that he is tired, and so on. If you insist that inquiry must go until a reason of Freud's sort has been found for every slip, you are expressing a determination to find that sort of explanation and to be content with it and with no other. What appears to be a healthy scepticism and hostility to chance as a factor in human affairs is in reality a blind prejudice in favour of one kind of account. This can be seen from the fact that, even if we conceive it as a causal explanation, the Freudian explanation of slips must also leave room for chance: it cannot hope to explain why just these Freudian slips and no others were made. Like every other form of explanation it must say, "Well, conditions just happened to favour these particular slips."

The plausibility of the explanations given by Freud, the reconstructions made in the course of them, and so on do not show that a whole area of causation has been laid bare here. In line with our previous remarks drawn from Wittgenstein these factors show rather that a process of free association and judicious questioning by the analyst will nearly always lead to matters of central concern to the subject.

Here, starting from the supposed scientific character of the explanation given, we arrive instead at an insight into its mythological nature. Everything has an explanation, everything is significant: this is not the expression of a scientific attitude but of a primitive one. A chance conjuncture tells us something – birds flying into a certain area of sky from the right or from the left tell us who will win a forthcoming battle. The position of the stars at the moment of a man's birth is not accidentally connected with his fortunes. Divination and astrology are for most of us defunct practices, but we can understand what their function was in many ways. The need to see a meaning in everything, the need to have some *ratio decidendi* in obscure but important questions, the need to have some account or other of why things happen to a man, some rationalization of it. It may be that any reflection on the human condition, such as astrology must involve, will reveal something to us. Or it may help one to have an account of what one is likely to do, so as to guide one in life, rather as Wallenstein is thought to have lived out as if on purpose the remarkably accurate prediction made by Kepler. Astrology, witchcraft, and magic may favour and encourage certain forms of life; they may be necessary for certain people. And usually we can understand their need even if we do not feel it.

Wittgenstein wrote more than once during the 1930s about magic and ritual, principally in connection with his reading of Frazer's *Golden Bough*. This was part of the ethnological or anthropological way of looking at things that came to him from the economist Sraffa and that he regarded as one of the most fruitful lessons of those years. (Some of the remarks on Frazer are printed in *Synthese* 17 (1967) and translated in *The Human World* (1971).) It is important to understand Wittgenstein's attitude towards this pervasive phenomenon. Religious and magical ways of thinking and acting do not rest on false scientific beliefs (nor on true ones either). They are not given up or changed simply when some matter of fact is pointed out to those concerned. Moreover, our lives too and our thinking, not merely those of primitive peoples, have much ritual in them and much mythology (it is there indeed that philosophy has its origin, according to Wittgenstein). Its essence may be seen clearly enough in small things such as kissing the picture of the beloved or striking some inanimate object when angry.

> When I am furious about something, I sometimes hit the ground or a tree with my stick, and the like. But I certainly don't think that the ground is to blame or that this hitting can help at all. "I give vent to my anger." And that is what all rites are like. Such actions could be called instinctive actions. – And a historical explanation, e.g. that in the past I or my ancestors used to believe that it helped to strike the ground is humbug, because it is a superfluous assumption that explains nothing. The important thing is the similarity with an act of punishing, but nothing more than similarity is to be found.
>
> Once such a phenomenon has been brought into a relation with an instinct we ourselves possess, that alone is the desired solution, i.e. the solution that resolves this particular difficulty. Any further research into the history of my instincts would follow quite different paths. (*Synthese* 17 (1967), p. 244; omitted in *The Human World* version)

Similarly, understanding the ritual of a primitive people involves bringing in an inclination we ourselves feel. And this is nearly always possible: it is as if we have already in our minds the principle underlying the whole diversity of primitive usages. "The inner nature" of a ritual, "the inner life of thought and feeling" that accompanies it is something familiar to us. We feel that we could invent primitive usages and that it would be a mere accident if they were nowhere found in reality. (This is

quite consistent with the point he also makes that festivals such
as Beltane are not free inventions of man.)

This brings us back to Freud and to Wittgenstein's view of his
achievement. Freud invented, on that view, a way of thinking
and talking and a life associated with it, which corresponded
with something universal in the human spirit (and which
therefore easily fitted many pre-existing myths). So far as the
statements made in the exposition of this way of thinking were
taken as scientific, Freud or his followers fell into error, the same
sort of error that is made when magic is analysed scientifically.
(This parallel, I must point out, is my contribution.) But if this
error was not made – what then? First, something illuminating
had been done by the very demonstration of the possibility of
this way of thinking. Second, if it were adopted and followed in
a consequential manner, a certain impoverishment of our
mental life – a shrinking, if one may so term it, to a single one of
the many possibilities of development – would ensue. Third, a
man might still learn a lot about himself by adopting it, that is,
by undergoing analysis, but he would at the same time have to
resist the strength of the mythology – to see it, I suppose this
means, as only one of the ways of thinking about these matters.
On a small scale this would amount to seeing that dreams and
slips may not *all* serve a single purpose or follow a single pattern.
I compare this with the savage, who, as Wittgenstein says, "to
all appearance sticks pins in his enemy's picture in order to kill
him, but also builds his hut with real wood and cuts himself an
arrow skilfully and not in effigy." (*Synthese* 17 (1967) p. 237;
The Human World, 3 (1971), p. 31; the present translation,
however, is mine).

The above is not intended as a casting-up of accounts on
Freud, which it would be ridiculous to attempt on the basis of a
few scattered insights, interesting though I find them, in
Wittgenstein. It will serve though to introduce the question
why and with what justice Wittgenstein regarded himself as a

follower of Freud's. Discussion of the point may throw light on
both thinkers.

For a while after World War II it was fashionable to refer to
Wittgenstein's work as "therapeutic positivism" (B. Farrell, M.
Lazerowitz). The noun is certainly unfortunate: the original
positivists wanted all thinking to follow the pattern of natural
science, whereas even in his first work Wittgenstein's aim was
to show that large areas of human concern were not accessible to
science. When he returned to philosophy in the 1930s, his *bête
noire* was the attempt, say, of Jeans and Eddington to reach a
world-view through science. He thought of his own work (as
appears from the preface composed in 1930 and now printed
with his *Philosophical Remarks*) as written in a spirit quite
different from that of the age: the spirit of the age was one of
confidence in progress and in science (it is interesting that the
motto to his *Philosophical Investigations*, chosen probably round
1945, is also expressive of distrust in progress). His aim was a
profounder understanding rather than any progress. All the
moral and social problems that we faced were not even touched
by science. Not that there was anything wrong with science,
only with its status in our culture. We needed a change in
culture. Here, in his anti-positivism, Wittgenstein was indebted
both to Freud and Sraffa, to Freud for the vision of how a
problem could (though with great difficulty) be taken up by the
roots and put into a quite new way of thinking, to Sraffa for the
idea of a way of thinking as reflecting the character of a culture.
(I speak of where he actually got these ideas from – he could no
doubt have learnt more from Freud if he had read more than the
pre-World War I works.)

Though his work was thus no positivism, there were grounds
for calling it therapeutic. He himself was a little annoyed by the
idea. "When you think of the investigation of philosophical
problems as a form of psychoanalysis, you think like a phys-
ician – 'We'll soon put that right!'" (reported conversation

with R. Rhees). Perhaps some who made the comparison did think of the "dissolution" of philosophical problems (compare the decomposition of the dream of which Wittgenstein spoke) as proceeding rapidly – whereas Wittgenstein thought that the source of philosophical problems was so deeply rooted in our thinking that any advance would be very slow. The advance that he thought possible was to be made by the individual, and here Wittgenstein himself drew the analogy with psychoanalysis: the individual was to be the judge of success, that is, relative to himself. The philosopher is plagued by a problem. Some expression disturbs him, seems to demand to be used in a certain way which he cannot quite allow (we shall see an example shortly). He has to find a context in which the disturbing expression is at home. When its full context is shown, it is no longer problematic. This is where a lesson learnt from Freud that we have already mentioned comes in: the idea that the meaning is not there all at once but is something that appears in the course of discussion, so that understanding is a process extended in time.

The philosopher is one with a susceptibility to certain so-called problems that are really the result of a muddle. He has a temptation to overcome:

> A philosopher has temptations which an ordinary person does not have. We *could* say he knows better what the word means than the others do. But actually philosophers generally know *less*. Because ordinary people have no temptations to misunderstand language. (Notes taken in Wittgenstein's lectures of summer term, 1936, by Rush Rhees)

Slightly earlier he thought that the difficulty was a resistance in the will. An heroic effort was required if metaphysics was to be given up, a revolution in our thinking, not only in the sense that we needed to turn round and look in the opposite direction (one of the hardest things in the world to do) but a revolution in the other sense, something like the Russian revolution. Wittgenstein thought that nothing was to be hoped for from Western culture: it was a thing of the past, its energy had been spent by about 1850: the only hope lay in Russia where everything had been destroyed. And a similar complete departure from former ways of thinking was required in philosophy too. He criticized his friend Ramsey for being a bourgeois thinker, not prepared for this complete renunciation. He himself felt that he was writing for a future race, for people who would think in a totally different way. Here his kinship with Nietzsche is very evident.

What we have to break loose from in the first place is metaphysics, a bewitchment by language and its forms, which lead us to make statements which have all the form of empirical or factual statements, but which we know to be not statements of fact at all. Such are the statements of Wittgenstein's own first book, in which he talks about the form of the world and the way it is mirrored in language as if such entities existed and stood in relations to one another just like those of solid everyday objects. We have the idea as we read the book that it contains the results of a super-science which gives us the most general laws. Of course that book does end with the insight that its own propositions are nonsensical, but it is a testimony to the attractiveness of a certain picture. We feel that language is a system which is there to be talked about, whereas we cannot describe language or thought by one formula, but can only exhibit the sorts of thing we can do with it in practice. Another example (quoted by Rhees below in his discussion of language and ritual) concerns the phrase "I meant him" – the process of meaning or intending:

I say, "Please come here", and beckon to him. I meant A and not B. I did mean him, there is no doubt about that. And yet it seems to be clear that unless I want to fabricate something there was no connection between me (or my speaking) and him other than, say, my glance and the like. This "meaning him" construed as a connection is like a myth. And a very powerful myth. Because

whatever sort of connection I imagine, none of them does what I
want. No connection that I can imagine will be adequate, and
consequently it seems that meaning must be a specific connection
quite incomparable with all other forms of connection. (MS 116,
275, cited again below, p. 77)

If we look at the surface of our language it seems to demand a
simple referent for all such words – as if "meaning him" were
like "hitting him". And we even rather enjoy that way of
thinking about it, as Cantor enjoyed talking about the set of all
real numbers – and imagining it written down in a certain
order. We feel that by giving a name to something, or by performing operations on a set, we have mastered it, have got
beyond our inability to grasp it as something simple, to see it.
We obtain by these means, in our own estimation, an angel's
knowledge, and this pleases us. But of course we *ought not* to do
this. As Wittgenstein said about philosophy in a conversation
reported by R. Rhees: "I am not trying to get you to believe
something you don't believe but to do something you won't
do." What the philosopher ought to do is to draw attention to
the great multiplicity of things that are normally done, practices
of the group, which make it possible for me to "mean him".
That philosopher's question should be: "*When* do we say that
one person means another?" not, "*How* is it done?", because the
latter contains another surrender to the mythology implicit in
our speech-forms. ("Well it *is* after all a process . . . it must
either be going on or not.") This is not a mistake about the facts
of the case. 'Meaning' is indeed a process . . . -word, but it is a
mistake to be obsessed with this feature of our language, which
is of little importance, a philosophical mistake, which can have
the aim merely of feeding our vanity but can also help us to
avoid thinking clearly in important matters.

So Wittgenstein wants to avoid the mythology implicit in
our first reflections on language. He wants to substitute a form
of reflection which avoids it – though perhaps at the risk of

introducing a new mythology of its own, that of "use" as something present all at once, for example. He wants to see through the surface grammar of a word to its depth grammar. This (it seems to me) is what made it natural for him to call himself a pupil or follower of Freud, for he had in Freud an example of how a new and deeper but often less flattering interpretation could be substituted for the apparent meaning and at the same time of how a mythology could captivate. He accepted and rejected Freud in equal measure, perhaps healthily.

Wittgenstein's Later Work in relation to Conservatism*

J. C. Nyíri

The well-known fact that in Wittgenstein's later philosophy there is a tendency to emphasize the genetic, or historical, aspect of individual mental occurrences, and to regard these as manifestations of social customs and institutions, would not, in itself, justify the attempt to establish a relationship between this philosophy, and certain currents of conservatism. Yet the specific tone of Wittgenstein's analyses, the content of many of his remarks and reflections, and the historical circumstances in which this philosophy came into being definitely invite an interpretation in the light of which there indeed emerge family resemblances between Wittgenstein on the one hand and some important representatives of conservatism on the other. Conservative ideas do not, of course, form a unified and coherent whole; an interpretation along the lines here indicated will present only rough outlines, not a sharp picture – especially

* The present paper is an attempt to elaborate historically some theses which were put forward in my paper "Wittgenstein's New Traditionalism" in *Essays on Wittgenstein in Honour of G. H. von Wright* (*Acta Philosophica Fennica*, 28, nos. 1–2, pp. 501–512), and in my paper read at the 2nd International Wittgenstein Symposium, 1977, Kirchberg am Wechsel (see *Wittgenstein and His Impact on Contemporary Thought*, Hölder-Pichler-Tempsky, Vienna, 1978, pp. 36–41). I am greatly indebted to Professor G. H. von Wright for his constant help and encouragement, to Dr Lars Hertzberg (Helsinki) for sympathetic criticism and to Dr Barry Smith (Manchester) for valuable bibliographical references.
Further notes on this paper will be found on pp. 64–8.

since Wittgenstein's position in respect to the body of conservative literature cannot be satisfactorily determined in the absence of a thorough analysis of his unpublished manuscripts.[1] Still, the interpretation here presented, even if merely an approximation, seems to me to constitute a necessary step towards a more complete picture of Wittgenstein's philosophy. Wittgenstein's later philosophy emerged at a time when conservatism – in the form of neo-conservatism – was one of the dominant spiritual currents in Germany and Austria; and Wittgenstein received decisive impulses both from authors who deeply influenced this current and from representatives of the new conservatism itself. Moreover, Wittgenstein dealt with problems which were fundamental problems also of contemporary neo-conservatism – albeit in a manner which was, of course, far deeper and more rigorous than that of the leading neo-conservatives of his day – and he succeeded further in solving these problems, in so far as they were theoretically solvable at all. Any presentation of Wittgenstein's later work that does not allow for these historical and systematic parallels must remain essentially incomplete.

In presenting the later Wittgenstein as belonging to a constellation of conservative thinkers, I shall partly recall influences that are well known but are generally neither sufficiently recognized nor properly interpreted; partly refer to influences and parallels which have hitherto apparently gone unnoticed; and partly point to certain parallel which are, presumably, independent of any direct influence – but which precisely for this reason have, perhaps, an even greater significance. Let me first, however, draw attention to certain problems pertaining to the concept and to the history of conservatism.

The term 'conservative' is used in at least three types of context. People speak of a conservative attitude or mentality, of conservative theory, and of conservative politics. Conservative attitude, theory, and politics are of course by no means independent of each other. Conservative theory comes into being, in certain social and historical circumstances, as an abstract self-perception of conservative mentality, presenting the latter as the only acceptable or indeed normal one. Conservative theory can take the form of anthropology, social theory, or the theory of history; in its content it can embody very different tendencies, depending on what remains – if anything at all – that is regarded as worth conserving, or even re-establishing. Conservative politics, finally, are upheld by conservative mentality, and directed by conservative theory – though this latter relationship is already a rather difficult one, since conservative mentality and thus also conservative politics have a distaste for any theory. A conservative political creed as such does not exist, and conservative politics change with the times; many of today's conservative aims correspond to liberal ideas of yesterday.

Let us consider more closely the essence of conservative mentality, the source of everything conservative. As recently formulated by Gerd-Klaus Kaltenbrunner, the man of conservative character is

devoted to the familiar and mistrustful of all novelties; he holds on to that which obtains, to that which has been tried and tested; he has a decisive preference for the experiences of life as opposed to the constructions of the intellect, and affirms instinctively the durable, the constant, the traditional; he is sceptical of every radicalism, of utopias, and of promises in regard to the future; he always begins with that which is concrete, and would rather underestimate than overestimate his fellow men. . . .[2]

According to Michael Oakeshott, the well-known English conservative theorist, to be conservative means to have "a propensity to use and to enjoy what is available rather than to wish for or to look for something else; to delight in what is present rather than what was or what may be". To be conservative means to be "equal to one's own fortune, to live at the level of one's own means, to be content with the want of greater perfection which belongs alike to oneself and one's circumstances".[3] Yet Oakeshott also observes that in an "arid", unpleasant world, "if the present is remarkably unsettled", the conservative attitude will transform itself into "a search for a firmer foothold", becoming "a recourse to and an exploration of the past".[4] This is the birth of conservatism as a theory out of conservatism as an attitude. As Karl Mannheim formulated it:

> The simple habit of living more or less unconsciously, as though the old ways of life were still appropriate, gradually gives way to a deliberate effort to maintain them under the new conditions, and they are raised to the level of conscious reflection, of deliberate "recollection". Conservative thought thus saves itself, so to speak, by raising to the level of reflection and conscious manipulation those forms of experience which can no longer be had in an authentic way.[5]

This very transformation of forms of experience into theory occurs with the emergence of the conservative reaction against the French Revolution and French rationalism; but also with the emergence of Austrian and German neo-conservatism during and after World War I. It is a characteristic trait of conservative theory that it only emerges in a battle against other theories, theories which typically preach the power of theory, the power of the mind. Conservative theory, preferring the given and the concrete, is always hostile towards any theory as such. Conservatism, as Armin Mohler writes, "congeals into a theory only when a point is reached where it must defend itself against some opposing theory".[6] The most radical expression of the conservative hostility against theory is the distaste for all abstract concepts: the conservative preference for silence. Mohler writes of the "peculiar dumbness with which everything conservative is stamped".[7] This silence seems to become ever more compelling as the distance grows between contemporary reality and the order of the past – the order that is to be re-established. But, at the same time, the need to possess a guiding theory becomes ever more compelling. The so-called old conservatism of the nineteenth-century spoke simply of an historically developed or indeed divine order which was to be preserved or re-erected. But the German and Austrian neo-conservatives of the twenties and early thirties were no longer acquainted with any traditions that would have been worth preserving; they wanted change, without however knowing – or being able to know – in what direction this change should occur. As K. von Klemperer puts it, "the new conservatism was clearly heading into a dilemma between conserving and destroying, between a positive attitude toward our civilization and nihilism".[8] The old conservatism had, philosophically speaking, an ontology as its basis; neo-conservatism, however, is a conservatism from which history has taken away the possibility of an ontology.

There can be no doubt that both in his youth and in his later years conservative attitudes were strongly characteristic of Wittgenstein. It was not by chance that, in his student days, he so very much disliked the lack of reverence displayed by his friends at Cambridge.[9] Paul Engelmann speaks of his "loyalty towards all legitimate authority, whether religious or social", an attitude "towards all *genuine* authority [which] was so much second nature with him that revolutionary convictions of whatever kind appeared to him throughout his life simply as 'immoral'".[10] The young Wittgenstein, writes Engelmann, "suffered acutely under the discrepancy between the world as it is and as it ought to be according to his light, but . . . tended also to seek the source of that discrepancy within, rather than outside, himself". And, he goes on, "the person who consistently believes that the reason for the discrepancy lies in himself alone must reject the belief that changes in the external facts may be necessary and called for".[11] Wittgenstein's conservative attitude is strikingly expressed in his dislike for any language that has not "grown organically";[12] or in his often voiced disparaging judgement of modern art, especially architecture.[13]

It seems to me that already in the *Tractatus* this attitude had become crystallized into a kind of conservative theory. Yet the conservatism of Wittgenstein's later philosophy is more direct, more pronounced. Its emergence was fostered, first and foremost, by his experiences of the post-war period – experiences of a world-order that had vanished and of deepest homelessness. What Franz Theodor Csokor said of Musil, namely that by the year 1918 he had actually lost his homeland and that he had thereafter sought to re-erect it in his work,[14] applies equally to Wittgenstein. And although it was only after 1930 that Wittgenstein's later philosophy came into being, already in the twenties some of its fundamental features had emerged. A conservative author who at this time obviously had a profound influence on Wittgenstein was the Russian writer F. M. Dostoevsky.

Wittgenstein's admiration for Dostoevsky is well known. One finds important references to it in the writings of Russell,[15] Engelmann,[16] von Wright,[17] Norman Malcolm,[18] and also in Fania Pascal's recollections.[19] M. O'C. Drury quotes Wittgenstein as saying that when he was a village schoolmaster in Lower Austria during the first half of the twenties, he read the *Brothers Karamazov* over and over again, even reading it out loud to the village priest.[20] Some of the references emphasize that Wittgenstein was particularly fascinated by the figure of the Elder Zossima. The orthodox institution of the Elders is, according to Dostoevsky's description, a most strictly authoritarian one. When you select an Elder, a religious-spiritual guide for yourself, "you renounce your own will and yield it to him in complete submission, complete self-abnegation. . . . This terrible school of abnegation is undertaken . . . in order, after a life of obedience, to attain perfect freedom" – to escape the burden of spiritual unrestraint.[21]

The idea that true freedom – even that of the spirit – cannot

but consist in a kind of restraint, is of course one of the basic ideas of conservatism. It influences Wittgenstein's later philosophy in many ways, but can already by discerned in the (originally unprinted) introduction to the booklet *Wörterbuch für Volksschulen*, published in 1926. The aim of this dictionary was "to enable students to inform themselves about the spelling of a word" – for only a dictionary, as Wittgenstein stressed, "makes it possible to hold the student completely responsible for the spelling of what he has written": only through fixed rules can the "orthographic conscience" be awakened.[22] That one must "recognize certain authorities in order to make judgements at all", or that one cannot even err – that is, that one loses altogether the capacity for rational thought – if one does not *judge in conformity*[23] with some group or other: such views, worked out in detail in his later philosophy, were obviously already characteristic of the Wittgenstein of the twenties.

It would be interesting to know which edition of the *Brothers Karamazov* Wittgenstein possessed in the twenties. I assume that it was the edition published by Piper Verlag, in the series Dostoevsky's *Sämtliche Werke*. These were edited by Moeller van den Bruck, a leading German neo-conservative thinker, and co-edited by Dmitri Mereschkowski, who wrote the introduction to the *Brothers Karamazov*. The principal concern of Dostoevsky (and of Tolstoy), which is identical with "the principal concern of the whole of Christianity", is, Mereschkowski here suggests, a concern with the "end of the world". "I feel the danger threatening me", remarks Mereschkowski, "of making ridiculous that which is most holy, since for the children of this century, the men of constant mediocrity, of endless 'progress', and 'development' in the world, there is nothing more ridiculous, more stupid, more improbable, more offensive" – than the thought of the end of the world.[24] To Wittgenstein, however, this thought did not seem at all ridiculous;[25] and his distaste for modes of thinking "characterized by the word 'progress'"[26] is later unequivocally expressed in drafts for a foreword to a book he planned in 1930.[27]

The neo-conservative Dostoevsky interpretation certainly also played a role in connection with Wittgenstein's well-known yearning for Russia.[28] "What we need in Germany is Russia's unqualified spirituality. We need this as a counterweight against a West to whose influences we have been exposed as Russia was exposed, a West that has brought us to this state in which we now find ourselves." Thus run the opening sentences of Moeller van den Bruck's introduction to Dostoevsky's *Crime and Punishment* in the edition of 1922. The idea that German conservatism, in its transvaluation of all Western values, cannot but turn to the spiritual reserves of Russianism is an idea which constantly recurs in Moeller's writings;[29] he himself made a journey to Russia in 1912. And this same contrast between Russia and the degenerate Western civilization is of course a subject which we repeatedly encounter in the writings of Spengler. Spengler was probably the most influential neo-conservative thinker of the post-war years, and that he had an essential influence on Wittgenstein during the very time Wittgenstein's later philosophy actually emerged – that is, in 1931 – must now, with the publication of *Culture and Value*, be plainly apparent.

One well-known passage in which Wittgenstein mentions Spengler, is contained in his "Remarks on Frazer's *The Golden Bough*", written in 1931.[30] But there is another German conservative author who is referred to in the manuscripts from which these "Remarks" were selected: the playwright and essayist Paul Ernst. "Should my book ever be published", wrote Wittgenstein, "its foreword must contain an acknowledgement to the Foreword of Paul Ernst to his edition of *Grimms' Fairy Tales*, which Foreword I should have acknowledged already in the *Log. Phil. Abhandlung*, as the source of the expression 'misunderstanding the logic of language'."[31] And in the so-called Big Typescript (dictated probably in 1933) we find, functioning as a sub-title to some passages on Frazer, the sentence: "Mythology in the forms of our language ((Paul Ernst))." The "Foreword" of Ernst, to which Wittgenstein refers, is actually a postscript in the third volume of Ernst's edition of the *Grimmsche Kinder- und Hausmärchen*,[32] where Ernst writes of magical-mythological conceptions arising "from the interpretation of a misunderstood tendency of language" and of "changes in language" accompanied by changes in the "logic of language"[33] – formulae that must have been important not only to the author of the *Tractatus*,[34] but indeed to the later Wittgenstein as well. It is possible also that some other formulations which Ernst here applies had an effect on Wittgenstein, perhaps especially on the methodology underlying his comments on Frazer.[35] And the last pages of the postscript contain remarks on Tolstoy and Dostoevsky with which Wittgenstein must certainly have agreed, for example with the remark that Tolstoy's "newly invented legends" – obviously, the *Folk Tales* – belong "to the most beautiful works of the human spirit", and might "live for thousands of years, not just as themes, but in the very form which Tolstoy gave them".[36]

Whether Wittgenstein ever read anything by Paul Ernst other than this postscript cannot be decided on the basis of the material available to me.[37] But I consider it appropriate and necessary to refer here in some detail to the theoretical position which was maintained by Ernst in the late twenties, especially since this position – and Ernst's work generally – was certainly not without influence in contemporary Germany. I select his essay "What Now?", published in 1926/27.[38] This work, which begins, incidentally, with what is an obviously not wholly justified attack on Spengler,[39] deals with the foundations and functions of poetry under "organic" and "unorganic" forms of life. "As a result of the faint awareness", writes Ernst, "that in the disintegration of today" it is almost the peasant alone who "still possesses an organic mode of life, there arises, as is always the case in times of dissolution, a peasant poetry. This does not, however, emanate from the peasantry, but from members of the other orders."[40] Ernst then argues that, like that of the peasant, "so also is the form of life of the master an organic one, a form which imbues the whole man".[41] And "only when the life of the master becomes questionable as other forms of life have come to appear possible . . . does there arise a master-poetry".[42] The "unorganic forms of life" Ernst brings together under the term "bourgeois".

> All those forms of life are bourgeois which imbue not the whole man but merely some part of him, and it is within those forms that terms such as profession and status, work and personality, have acquired their contemporary meaning. Here the life of the individual is no longer settled in a natural way, it is no longer simply determined by fixed consitions, like the life of the bees; it must be formed anew at every occasion, and everyone must search for this form himself.[43]

Ernst believes that the present is characterized throughout by the bourgeois form of life. "It is very clear where man today stands socially. Through the civilization of the last three hundred years an unorganic condition has been created, such as the world has hitherto never seen."[44] Men have now been "freed of every form-creating constraint, and have been left completely on their own. And it is clear that nothing can come of this except senseless barbarism. – Thus because man needs form and constraint he has come to feel profoundly unhappy, and the yearning which had already arisen amongst the old bourgeois as a result of the schism between culture and reality has acquired a vastly greater power."[45] And "when men live almost completely unorganically, when society has been almost completely dissolved . . . then God can no longer manifest himself in society as, in good times, he manifests himself in the state, in the church, in discipline and in customs. He manifests himself instead in the individual."[46]

The emergence of Wittgenstein's later philosophy is usually, and in a trivial sense correctly, attributed to his return to Cambridge in January 1929. But on the one hand two full years elapsed before Wittgenstein in Cambridge found the subjects and the style which were to become characteristic of his later period. On the other hand, the fact that it was in 1929 when he once more took up philosophy is something which itself stands in need of elucidation. Obviously, if one considers his external circumstances only, the same could just as well have taken place as early as in 1925, when Wittgenstein returned to England for the first time after the war. It appears that Wittgenstein's return to philosophy and the emergence of his later mode of thinking, must be regarded in a broader historical context, the context of the heyday and collapse of Austrian and German neo-conservatism between 1927 and 1933. The economic and political causes of the relevant developments – the economic crisis, beginning in 1929 and culminating in 1931,[47] and the political defeat of the German neo-conservatives with Hitler's rise to power – can only be mentioned her. But I would like to describe in some detail the neo-conservative spiritual milieu of the time. It seems to be natural to begin this description with a reference to the famous speech given by the Austrian poet Hugo von Hofmannsthal on 10 January 1927, before the students of the University of Munich. He spoke of a process which has advanced in "our questing German mind" – the mind of a people which "for centuries has been no longer rooted in its culture" – a process guided by the knowledge that "life becomes livable only through a system of genuine obligations." This process arose as "an internal opposing force counter to that spiritual upheaval of the sixteenth century which, in its two aspects, we tend to call renaissance and reformation. The process of which I speak is", said Hofmannsthal, "nothing other than a conservative revolution of a magnitude which is hitherto unprecedented in the history of Europe."[48]

In the same year that Hofmannsthal delivered his Munich

speech the lawyer Theodor Böttiger, member of the conservative Berlin *Herrenklub*, published his book, *Variations on a Conservative Theme*. "The conservative", wrote Böttiger, "maintains the thesis that the sum of all human happiness on earth will remain always the same, whilst the believer in progress maintains that a heightening of all values is possible and lies within the power of mankind." But, he argued, no value is raised up without the sinking of another. "The most illuminating thought creates, somewhere, a new obscurity, every remedy creates some new illness, every new happiness some new craving. That there is progress in specific cases is impossible to deny, but seen as a whole, from high above, this is counteracted by a step backwards at some other point."[49] Robert Musil expressed a similar attitude in his novel published towards the end of 1930, when he wrote that all "progress means a gain in each particular case, but also a severance from the wholeness of things; and this means an increase in power, which leads to a progressive increase in powerlessness . . ."[50] In Spengler's *Der Mensch und die Technik*, published in 1931, the concept of progress was simply disposed of as the "great word of the last century".[51]

In March 1931 the prominent publicist Adolf Grabowsky, later a professor at Basel, published his paper "Conservatism", in which he spoke of an "unintellectual closeness to life" as being characteristic of the conservative attitude. He described this attitude as a natural trait of uncorrupted common sense, remarking, however, that the man of today is typically *not* conservative. One could indeed go so far as to say, wrote Grabowsky, "that they who do think as conservatives constitute a secret order, so secret, that they themselves have normally no idea of their association. However, just as soon as only three profound words have been exchanged, there is established a relationship, both mental and spiritual, within which it is unnecessary to waste words. . . . And thus perhaps for this reason a conservative is silent much more often than are the adherents of other views." A "silent reverence for the impenetrable" characterizes the conservative attitude, "not only is this reverence silent, however, but so also is that which is impenetrable, and thus our silent reverence is only a reflection of the great silence of all that is impenetrable". The latter, however, is nothing other than the "internal immobility" of all existence. Conservatism, Grabowsky wrote, "has a view of the world that reveals from the outside an incomparable agitation, but from the inside the deepest peace. . . . There is no progress in history, but there is, certainly, a divinity within the world." The religious and the conservative views of the world are, believes Grabowsky, not alien to each other: they are mediated by the concept of reverence – "a central concept of conservatism, the concept which perhaps most clearly distinguishes it from liberalism, democratism, and rationalism". The two world-views are, however, by no means identical. Religion (and Grabowsky is here speaking specifically of catholicism) "presupposes an objectively given and objectively determinable order of being and framework of values. Thus for the catholic truth itself is absolute, whilst knowledge of the truth is relative. For the conservative, the core is not any eternal truth. . . . One could perhaps say that the catholic concept of truth is replaced, within conservatism, by a concept still by far insufficiently discussed: the concept of ceremoniousness."[52]

In these last-quoted lines of Grabowsky the paradox of the neo-conservative position is very clearly manifested. His insight is that on the one hand man, by his very nature, cannot do without absolute standards, that he needs and ought to observe fixed truths, but that on the other hand all absolute standards have perished historically, are a thing of the past, and fixed truths do not exist at all. This leads to a logical – and emotional – difficulty which is hardly solvable by references to the (otherwise very suggestive) concept of "ceremoniousness". The concept of festive, ceremonious behaviour, of behaviour directed by unalterable rules which could, at the same time, have been quite different, plays of course a central role in, for example, Wittgenstein's comments on Frazer. But in order to bring the logical-anthropological problems surrounding this concept nearer to a solution deeper conceptual analyses were needed. And it is precisely such analyses which, in my opinion, Wittgenstein eventually provided. He saved, as it were, the neo-conservative position from a theoretical catastrophe at a time when, in Germany, it could no longer be saved from a political catastrophe.

Late in 1930 Wittgenstein prepared a draft for a foreword to the book he was planning to write at the time. This draft is something which belongs very clearly to the historical context referred to above and I wish to quote the relevant lines at some length.

> This book is written for those who are in sympathy with the spirit in which it is written. This is not, I believe, the spirit of the main current of European and American civilization. The spirit of this civilization makes itself manifest in the industry, architecture and music of our time, in its fascism and socialism, and it is alien and uncongenial to the author. This is not a value judgement. It is not, it is true, as though he accepted what nowadays passes for architecture as architecture or did not approach what is called modern music with the greatest suspicion (though without understanding its language), but still, the disappearance of the arts does not justify judging disparagingly the human beings who make up this civilization. For in times like these, genuine strong characters simply leave the arts aside and to turn to other things and somehow the worth of the individual man finds expression. Not, to be sure, in the way it would at a time of high culture. A culture is like a big organization which assigns each of its members a place where he can work in the spirit of the whole; and it is perfectly fair for his power to be measured by the contribution he succeeds in making to the whole enterprise. In an age without culture on the other hand forces become fragmented and the power of an individual man is used up in overcoming opposing forces and frictional resistances.[53]

These lines ought clearly to be viewed less as the foreword to
Wittgenstein's *Philosophical Remarks*, as drafted in 1929–30,
than as a prologue to the life-long analytical work which
he began precisely at this point. The concept which perhaps
occupies the most central place in the relevant analyses is
that of following a rule. Now the idea that human behaviour,
human speech, and human thought are not, as it were, free-
floating but are, on the contrary, constrained by rules, is in itself
by no means necessarily a conservative idea. For rules have to be
applied, and since they can neither determine their own application, nor be endlessly supported by rules of application, the
phenomenon of rule-following seems to point directly to an underlying region of arbitrariness, of irregularity, to a level at
which "everything could be justified",[54] since whatever one
does "can . . . be brought into accord with the rule",[55] "can be
interpreted as a consequence".[56] But Wittgenstein's
philosophical achievement was that he supplanted the conceptual framework within which this so to speak anarchistic conclusion can occur, by elaborating another, essentially different
one. The basic concepts of the new framework are: training and
behaviour, use, custom, institution, practice, technique, agreement. The following of a rule is a custom, an institution,
embedded in the agreements, in the correspondences of
behaviour within society. The question concerning the interpretation of any rule can be raised – though it need not be – and
it should be answered by referring to agreements in behaviour.
Rule-following is, in the last analysis, blind: it cannot be
explained or justified. And Wittgenstein again and again
emphasizes that the agreements which constitute a necessary
precondition of all order, all logic and communication through
language, and therefore also indeed of thinking in general, are
"not an agreement of *beliefs*",[57] but agreements, regularities in
the *foundations of judgement*,[58] in the "common behaviour of
mankind".[59] Thus although any given form of life, mode of
thought and behaviour, can be superseded by or have superim-

posed upon itself other forms of life, it cannot actually be criticized. All criticism presupposes a form of life, a language, that is, a tradition of agreements; every judgement is necessarily embedded in traditions. That is why traditions cannot be judged. "One can only *describe* here" Wittgenstein wrote in 1931 "and say: this is what human life is like."[60]

Thus the familiar passages in which Wittgenstein refers, for example, to "the sickness of a time" which cannot be cured by purposeful action,[61] or to an "order"[62] that is introduced without having been intended – are not chance remarks embedded within contexts which actually deal with other, quite different problems; they are, rather, exegetic guideposts. All the time Wittgenstein strives to show that the given form of life is the ultimate givenness, that the given form of life cannot be consciously transcended. Wittgenstein is of course perfectly aware of the fact that there are different forms of life, different ultimate givennesses. And that these different forms of life all have the same value, that human nature can manifest itself equally in various forms of life. But there is a human nature, since it is an unalterable anthropological fact – a fact,that is, indeed, a precondition for the existence of logic – that any human being must, in order to be a human being, be constrained by some form of life, by some network of tradition.

Wittgenstein's solution to the neo-conservative paradox was his insight that the possibility of other orders does not in the least weaken the inexorable binding force of our own, although autonomous changes in the latter might of course very well occur. This can very clearly be illustrated by those analyses which one could perhaps call Wittgenstein's sketch of *a theory of mental illness*. These analyses deal mostly with questions pertaining to the following of mathematical rules. Supposing, for example, that someone does not follow the usual rules of counting. The question we must first decide is whether what we have here is just plain error, or a case of mental disorder. And Wittgenstein's introductory answer of course is that there is no sharp line between an abnormal condition and the normal one.[63] Yet if the errors become very frequent, the boundary must clearly be regarded as having been overstepped. Now in such cases, where the necessary conformity does not obtain, we can distinguish again two possibilities: the deviations involved are either systematic, or random. Here, too, there is no sharp distinction,[64] but clear cases can certainly be discerned. And if someone constantly commits random mistakes, if rules have lost all significance for him, then, indeed, he himself must be regarded as mentally lost, as crazy.[65] Let us suppose, however, that the deviations from the rule have a systematic nature, that is, that someone's reactions are systematically different. In this case the terms 'mental disorder', 'insanity', 'madness', 'feeble-mindedness', are actually misleading, because we have an order here, even if it is an order different from our own. And it is important that the picture of a different order is always combined by Wittgenstein with the picture of a different society, that he therefore regards as truly sick only those modes of behaviour which would not count as normal in *any* society. "One imagines the feeble-minded", writes Wittgenstein in the mid-forties, "under the aspect of the degenerate, the essentially incomplete, as it were in tatters. And so under that of disorder instead of a more primitive order (which would be a far more fruitful way of looking at them). – We just don't see a *society* of such people. – What would a society consisting solely of deaf men be like? Or a society of the 'feeble-minded'? *An important question!* What would, that is, a society be like that never played many of our customary language-games?"[66] If in our culture, Wittgenstein remarks in 1936, "a child does not perform the transition '20' – '21' upon the suggestive gesture of the teacher, people will treat it as feeble-minded".[67] But one can very well imagine a tribe in the life of which a certain number, say 20, plays a peculiar role, namely that of "an insurmountable upper limit",[68] and here the above-mentioned child would of course count as normal. The decisive point however is that, all these considerations notwithstanding, we cannot entertain a liberal attitude as regards irregularities in our *own* society. For it is through compelling uniformities that the life of a society becomes ordered, such uniformities determine the boundaries of a society, that is, only through such uniformities does the society as such become constituted. A familiar passage in Wittgenstein's writings runs:

> We should presumably not call it 'counting' if everyone said the numbers one after the other *anyhow*; but of course it is not simply a question of a name. For what we call 'counting' is an important part of our life's activities. . . . Counting (and that means: counting like *this*) is a technique that is employed daily in the most various operations of our lives. And that is why we learn to count as we do: with endless practice, with merciless exactitude; that is why it is inexorably insisted that we shall all say 'two' after 'one', 'three' after 'two' and so on.[69]

Someone counting correctly hastens, as it were, "to a common meeting point with everybody else".[70] Our technique of counting, the system of rules in which we move, is of course not unalterable. But new rules would have to emerge from the old ones *organically*, so to speak. We switch over to a different technique "not because we tell ourselves that it will work this way too, but because we feel the new technique to be identical with the old one".[71]

That Wittgenstein's conceptual analyses can in fact be regarded as a kind of foundation of conservatism is manifested in an interesting way by a parallel which I will now, in conclusion, briefly describe. I am referring to the amazing similarity between certain reflections of Michael Oakeshott and those of Wittgenstein. Whether the distinguished philosopher of history and political scientist who taught at Cambridge between 1925 and 1940 and was active there also after 1945, in fact stood under the temporary influence of Wittgenstein, whether he ever attended Wittgenstein's lectures or studied the notes taken at these, cannot be decided on the basis of the material available to me. I am not aware of any reference to Wittgenstein in Oakeshott's writings; in the lists of Wittgenstein's students prepared by the Wittgenstein Archives in Tübingen[72] Oakeshott's name does not occur. On the other hand, Wittgenstein's dictations "The Blue Book" and "The Brown Book" were, as is well known, widely copied and were rather easily available, especially at Cambridge. The question of a possible or actual influence is, however, in the present context, almost without interest. For the fact that Wittgenstein's later philosophy definitely permits of a conservative interpretation is in any case sufficiently illustrated by the parallels in question.

The essays of Oakeshott with which we shall be concerned here were written towards the end of the 1940s. The main tenet of these essays is the criticism of rationalism in general, and of rationalism in politics in particular. Rationalism is, for Oakeshott, the view according to which human actions, society, and institutions can and ought to be planned and guided by an authority independent of them: autonomous reason. The rationalist, Oakeshott tells us, believes "in the open mind, the mind free from prejudice and its relic, habit. He believes that the unhindered human 'reason' (if only it can be brought to bear) is an infallible guide in political activity. Further he believes in argument as the technique and operation of 'reason'; the truth of an opinion and the 'rational' ground (not the use) of an institution is all that matters to him."[73] Oakeshott, in contrast to the rationalist, realizes that human activity "is always activity with a pattern", with a pattern which is not, however, "superimposed", but which is "inherent in the activity itself". Elements of this pattern, writes Oakeshott, "occasionally stand out with a relatively firm outline; and we call these elements customs, traditions, institutions, laws, etc."[74] The rationalist has a false picture of the mode in which reason influences our actions and, indeed, has a false picture of reason; he has a false picture of the way in which one learns and applies the rules guiding one's actions. Oakeshott writes:

> There will always remain something of a mystery about how a tradition of political behaviour is learned, and perhaps the only certainty is that there is no point at which learning it can properly be said to begin. The politics of a community are not less individual (and not more so) than its language, and they are learned and practised in the same manner. We do not begin to learn our native language by learning the alphabet, or by learning its grammar; we do not begin by learning words, but words in use.[75]

All knowledge is, fundamentally, practical knowledge: "its normal expression is in a customary or traditional way of doing things, or, simply, in practice." Practical knowledge can "neither be taught nor learned, but only imparted and acquired".[76] We cannot explain any rules to someone who does not already possess the ability to apply some rules; "the rules of a game" cannot be imparted to an empty mind.[77] Thinking and doing, thinking and speaking are not separate activities specifically influencing each other: "rationality" is "a quality of the conduct itself", "no action is by itself 'rational', or is 'rational' on account of something that has gone on before. . . . 'Rationality' is the certificate we give to any conduct which can maintain a place in the flow of sympathy, the coherence of activity, which composes a way of living".[78] To say that a man "has a desire for something is only another way of saying that he is being active in a certain manner", and when a poet, for example, is searching for an appropriate expression, he does not know what he wants to say until he has actually said it. "The 'corrections' he may make to his first attempt are not efforts to make words correspond more closely to an already formulated idea or to images already fully formed in his mind."[79]

It is hardly necessary to refer here to parallel passages in the writings of Wittgenstein – the reader must certainly have noticed likenesses both in content and in formulation. It is not only similarities which meet the eye, however, but also an important difference. The passages quoted from Oakeshott are the logical *starting points* of his arguments, they serve as premisses to large-scale conclusions about society and history. In the writings of Wittgenstein, however, the corresponding passages are themselves the conclusions, the *results* of penetrating, rigorous analyses. It is, I believe, in the implications of this difference that Wittgenstein's significance for conservatism consists.

NOTES

1 The appendix of Garth Hallett's *A Companion to Wittgenstein's "Philosophical Investigations"* (Cornell University Press, 1977), for example, lists many unpublished manuscript passages where representatives of conservatism are mentioned.

2 Gerd-Klaus Kaltenbrunner "Der schwierige Konservatismus", in G.-K. Kaltenbrunner (editor) *Rekonstruktion des Konservatismus* (Freiburg i.B., 1972), p. 35.

3 M. Oakeshott *Rationalism in Politics* (London, 1962), pp. 168f.

4 *ibid.*, p. 169.

5 Karl Mannheim "Conservative Thought", in P. Kecskemeti (editor) *Essays in Sociology and Social Psychology* (London, 1953), p. 115.

6 Armin Mohler *Die Konservative Revolution in Deutschland 1918–1932* (Stuttgart, 1950), p. 163.

7 *ibid.*, p. 162.

8 Klemens von Klemperer *Germany's New Conservatism: Its History and Dilemma in the Twentieth Century* (Princeton, N.J., 1957), p. 7.

9 "We had no respect", writes J. M. Keynes in his recollections, "My Early Beliefs", "for traditional wisdom or the restraints of custom. We lacked reverence, as [D. H.] Lawrence observed and as Ludwig [Wittgenstein] with justice also used to say – for everything and everyone." (J. M. Keynes *Two Memoirs* (London, 1949), p. 99.)

10 Paul Engelmann *Letters from Ludwig Wittgenstein with a Memoir* (Oxford, 1967), p. 121.

11 *ibid.*, pp. 74, 79. In 1946 Wittgenstein still manifested the same mentality: "If life becomes hard to bear we think of a change in our circumstances. But the most important and effective change, a change in our own attitude, hardly even occurs to us, and the resolution to take such a step is very difficult for us." (*Culture and Value*, p. 53.)

12 "I sometimes had the impression", writes Rudolf Carnap in his intellectual autobiography, "that the deliberately rational and unemotional attitude of the scientist and likewise any ideas which had the flavor of 'enlightenment' were repugnant to Wittgenstein. At our very first meeting with Wittgenstein, [in 1927] Schlick unfortunately mentioned that I was interested in the problem of an international language like Esperanto. As I had expected, Wittgenstein was definitely opposed to this idea. But I was surprised by the vehemence of his emotions. A language which had not 'grown organically' seemed to him not only useless but despicable." (Carnap's recollections are reprinted in K. T. Fann (editor) *Wittgenstein: The Man and his Philosophy* (New York, 1967), p. 35.) As late as 1946 Wittgenstein still speaks of a "feeling of disgust" that he experiences when thinking of Esperanto (*Culture and Value*, p. 52).

13 e.g. *Culture and Value*, pp. 6, 79.

14 Franz Theodor Csokar "Gedenkrede zu Robert Musils 80. Geburtstag", in Karl Dinklage (editor) *Robert Musil: Leben, Werk, Wirkung* (Zürich, 1960), p. 354.

15 In his letter to Lady Ottoline Morrell (20 Dec. 1919). See Ludwig Wittgenstein *Letters to Russell, Keynes and Moore* (Oxford, 1974), p. 82.

16 *ibid.*, p. 27; see also the corresponding remark of the editor *ibid.*

17 G. H. von Wright "Biographical Sketch", in Norman Malcolm *Ludwig Wittgenstein: A Memoir* (London, 1958), p. 21.

18 *ibid.*, p. 52. Wittgenstein, Malcolm tells us, "had read *The Brothers Karamazov* an extraordinary number of times; but he once said that *The House of the Dead* was Dostoievsky's greatest work."

19 Fania Pascal "Wittgenstein: A Personal Memoir", *Encounter* (August 1973) p. 27. Mrs Pascal was Wittgenstein's Russian teacher at Cambridge in the mid-thirties.

20 M. O'C. Drury "Some Notes on Conversations with Wittgenstein", in *Essays on Wittgenstein in Honour of G. H. von Wright* (*Acta Philosophica Fennica*, 28), p. 31.

21 I quote from the Munich edition of 1920 vol. 1, p. 43.

22 Ludwig Wittgenstein *Wörterbuch für Volksschulen*. Edited with an introduction by Adolf Hübner-Werner and Elisabeth Leinfellner (Vienna, 1977), pp. xxv, xxvii.

23 Ludwig Wittgenstein *On Certainty*, §493; cf. *ibid.*, §156.

24 *Die Brüder Karamasoff* (Munich, 1920), vol. 1, p. xiv.

25 "The notion of a last judgement", writes Engelmann, "was of profound

concern to him. 'When we meet again at the last judgement' was a recurrent phrase with him, which he used in many a conversation at a particularly momentous point. He would pronounce the words with an indescribably inward-gazing look in his eyes, his head bowed, the picture of a man stirred to his depths." (*Letters from Ludwig Wittgenstein* (Oxford, 1967), pp. 77f.)

26 *Culture and Value*, p. 7.

27 One of these drafts containing the significant sentence, "I would like to say 'This book is written to the glory of God', but nowadays that would be chicanery, that is, it would not be rightly understood", was eventually printed as a foreword to *Philosophische Bemerkungen* (*Philosophical Remarks*).

28 Culminating, in the autumn of 1935, in a journey there; cf. *Letters to Russell, Keynes and Moore*, pp. 132–137, and Fania Pascal's recollections.

29 His best-known books were *Das Recht der jungen Völker* (1919) and *Das dritte Reich* (1923). In 1933 Hans Schwarz edited a posthumous volume *Rechenschaft über Russland* (An Account of Russia). The author committed suicide in 1925.

30 *Synthese* 17 (1967), p. 241 (*The Human World* 3 (1971), p. 35).

31 Quoted by Rush Rhees "Wittgenstein on Language and Ritual", in *Essays on Wittgenstein in Honour of G. H. von Wright*, p. 469, see also below p. 76.

32 Berlin, n.d.

33 *ibid.*, vol 3, pp. 273, 308.

34 The manner in which the relevant ideas of Ernst may have influenced the argument of the *Tractatus* is examined in Brian McGuinness "Philosophy of Science in the *Tractatus*", in G. Granger (editor) *Wittgenstein et le problème d'une philosophie de la science* (Paris, 1971), pp. 9f.

35 Thus for example Ernst wrote that those "many possible myths which one could work out schematically", one would then "also find in reality" (*Grimmsche Kinder- und Hausmärchen*, vol. 3, p. 291. Wittgenstein believed that "one could very well invent primitive customs for oneself and it would have to be an accident if they were not somewhere or other really to be found" ("Bemerkungen", p. 238 (*Acta Philosophica Fennica*, 28)). Ernst talks of an "association of intuitions" (*Grimmsche Kinder- und Hausmärchen*, vol. 3, p. 272); Wittgenstein of an "association of practices" (*The Human World*, p. 32) (see pp. 98 and 104 below).

36 *Grimmsche Kinder- und Hausmärchen*, vol. 3, pp. 312f. "Those short stories of Tolstoy's will live for ever. They were written for all peoples", Wittgenstein once remarked to Drury ("Some Notes on Conversations with Wittgenstein", p. 31).

37 Engelmann tells about Wittgenstein's acquaintance (during the war)

with Max Zweig, and mentions that Zweig later came under the influence of Ernst (*Letters from Ludwig Wittgenstein*, p. 65). It is not altogether impossible that Wittgenstein, too, was to some extent aware of Ernst's theoretical development in the course of the twenties.

38 *Die Horen* 3, (1926/27), no. 2 "What Now?" was reprinted in K. A. Kutzbach (editor) *Paul Ernst und Georg Lukács* (Emsdetten, 1974). Page numbers refer to the latter volume.

39 "In what follows," writes Ernst, "thoughts occasionally occur which remind one of Spengler's arguments. Here we remark merely that Spengler's "culture" is a fiction, and that his manner of dealing with insights which had been possessed by others long before him – insights which for us today are fatefully important – is one of outrageous dilettantism." ("What Now?", p. 189)

40 *ibid.*, p. 190.

41 *ibid.*, p. 191

42 *ibid.*

43 *ibid.*, p. 193.

44 *ibid.*, p. 194

45 *ibid.*, p. 198.

46 *ibid.*, pp. 200f.

47 "The year 1928", writes Klemperer, "was the last year of the prosperity which had marked the German economy since 1924. . . . It was quite clearly an economic and political crisis. . . . The withdrawal of funds from abroad and the effect of the stock market crash in New York in 1929 had direct repercussions upon German industry as well as agriculture. The figures for the unemployed passed the two million margin for the first time in the winter of 1928–1929, and soared up to nearly six million at the end of 1931. . . . These were the days", continues Klemperer, "when Moeller van den Bruck was read, re-read, re-edited in popular editions, and all but canonized, when Spengler was eagerly debated. . . . The neo-conservatives were the intellectuals of the Right who pointed toward the long-range spiritual roots of the crisis." (*Germany's New Conservatism*, pp. 125 and 118ff.) 1931 was a year of deep crisis in England also; see the account given by R. Kirk *Eliot and his Age*, (New York, 1971), p. 183.

48 H. von Hofmannsthal "Das Schrifttum als geistiger Raum der Nation". I am quoting from the *Gesammelte Werke* (Frankfurt, 1955), vol. Prosa 4, pp. 411–413. The term "conservative revolution" occurs already in Thomas Mann's essay "Russische Anthologie" (1921); cf. Armin Mohler *Die Konservative Revolution*, p. 18.

49 Georg Quabbe [Theodor Böttiger] *Tar a Ri. Variationen über ein konservatives Thema*, (Berlin, 1927), pp. 116f.

50 Robert Musil, *The Man without Qualities* (St Albans, 1968) vol. I, p. 203.
    There are a number of interesting parallels between Musil and Wittgen-
    stein. I attempted to point out some of them in a talk given in 1975,
    published in *Literatur und Kritik*, 113 (April 1977), pp. 167–179.
51 *Der Mensch und die Technik* (Munich, 1931), p. 9.
52 Adolf Grabowsky "Konservatismus", *Zeitschrift für Politik*, 20 (March
    1931) no. 12. I quote from pages 773, 775, 778–780, 785.
53 *Culture and Value*, p. 6.
54 Ludwig Wittgenstein, *Bermerkungen über die Grundlagen der Mathematik*,
    Schriften 6 (Frankfurt, 1974), p. 342.
55 Ludwig Wittgenstein, *Philosophical Investigations*, I, §198.
56 *Grundlagen der Mathematik*, p. 341.
57 *ibid.*, p. 353.
58 *ibid.*, p. 350.
59 *Philosophical Investigations*, I, §206.
60 "Bemerkungen über Frazers *The Golden Bough*", p. 236 (*The Human
    World*, p. 30).
61 Ludwig Wittgenstein, *Remarks on the Foundations of Mathematics*, I, App.
    II–4.
62 *ibid.*, II–83.
63 Ludwig Wittgenstein, *Zettel*, §393.
64 *Philosphical Investigations*, I, §143.
65 *On Certainty*, §217.
66 *Zettel*, §§372, 371.
67 Ludwig Wittgenstein, *Eine Philosophische Betrachtung*, schriften 5.
    (Frankfurt, 1970), p. 137.
68 *ibid.*
69 *Remarks on the Foundations of Mathematics*, I–4.
70 *ibid.*, II–69.
71 *ibid* . III–36.
72 *Katalog zum Wittgenstein-Nachlass* (Februar 1978) Anhang 2.
73 M. Oakeshott, *Rationalism in Politics* (London, 1962), pp. 3f.
74 *ibid.*, p. 105.
75 *ibid.*, p. 129.
76 *ibid.*, p. 11.
77 *ibid.*, p. 12.
78 *ibid.*, p. 109.
79 *ibid.*, pp. 104, 72.

Wittgenstein on Language and Ritual

Rush Rhees

PART I

A

In his first set of comments on Frazer (June 1931) Wittgenstein wrote:

> We have in the ancient rites the use of a very highly developed gesture-language.

> And when I read Frazer I keep wanting to say: All these processes, these changes of meaning, – we have them here still in our word-language. If what is hidden in the last sheaf is called the Corn-wolf, but also the last sheaf itself and also the man who binds it, we recognize in this a movement of language with which we are perfectly familiar.*

Then follows in the manuscript: "Our language is an embodiment of ancient myths. And the ritual of the ancient myths was a language." Wittgenstein did not include this in his typescript, and so it was not printed. He had written something like it a few pages earlier: "A whole mythology is deposited in our language" (p. 35).

1. We can recognize in all these ritual "processes" the kind

---

* "Remarks on Frazer's *Golden Bough*", *The Human World*, 3 May 1971, p. 36; future references are to this translation. The original (including a few extra passages) appeared in *Synthese* 17 (1967) pp. 233–253.

of shifts in meaning or in grammar that we use constantly in figures of speech such as metonymy or personification in our own language. Anthropologists had noticed and written of this before Wittgenstein wrote these comments. This cannot have been his point in writing them.

2. "We have in the ancient rites the use of a very highly developed gesture-language." In the next sentence Wittgenstein speaks of the parallels in the forms (figures and constructions) in our "word-language". Once or twice it looks as though he took gestures to be more fundamental than words, since we rely on gestures in first teaching children to speak and we resort to gestures to make ourselves understood by people when neither they nor we understand a word of the other's language (as, perhaps, Columbus did in the West Indies). A year or two earlier he had distinguished "primary signs" or gestures (especially the gesture of pointing) and "secondary signs" or words as a matter generally "worth thinking over". About the time of these comments on Frazer he was formulating the criticisms of it in *Philosophical Grammar* (pp. 88ff.). For example:

> It sounds like a ridiculous truism to say that a man who thinks that gestures are the primitive signs underlying all others would not be able to replace an ordinary sentence by gestures. (p. 89)

And yet there is a difference between gestures and words, although it cannot be put in terms of "primary" and "secondary", or of 'necessary' and 'arbitrary' (which sounds like trying to *explain* language, on analogy with elementary particles in physics). If Wittgenstein still thought of gestures as having a more general role than words, this was probably what, in *Philosophical Investigations* §206, is found "the common behaviour of mankind":

> Suppose you came as an explorer into an unknown country with

a language quite strange to you. In what circumstances would you say that the people there gave orders, understood them, obeyed them, rebelled against them, and so on?

The common behaviour of mankind is the system of reference by means of which we interpret an unknown language.

The difference is that the behaviour of mankind is not a system of signs, as gestures are. And at the time of the comments on Frazer Wittgenstein would have said that he could not have understood the gestures of a people whose language was totally strange to him. "Chinese gestures are as unintelligible to us as Chinese sentences." The sentence occurs in the same manuscript as the first set of comments on Frazer, in a passage that begins:

Understanding negation is seeing the defensive gesture in it.

Or: understanding negation is the same as understanding a defensive gesture. . . .

We can say, I can imagine seeing this gesture and not feeling it to be "defensive". For just in themselves the hand stretched out and the body leant back are no more defensive than a chair or a water-jug. . . .

And now I want to say this: it is not the fault of this particular movement that it is not in itself a defensive gesture. No! a movement as such is never a gesture. . . . Gesture language is a *language* and we have not in the ordinary sense learnt it. That is to say, it has not been (intentionally) deliberately taught us. And yet we have learnt it.

Chinese gestures are as unintelligible to us as Chinese sentences. (MS 110, 120–1)

About half a dozen years later (1937, probably) he wrote:

What makes a shrug a sign? . . .

Shrugs, shakes of the head, nods, etc. are called signs principally

because they are embedded in the way we use our spoken
language. (MS 116, 262)

3. The gestures made in those rituals had been learned in the
daily life and language of those who made them – or many, and
probably most of them, were. The gestures used *only* in
ceremony had their role as gestures – they were seen as gestures
– through some affinity with the gestures made in daily life and
practical affairs (in building, planting, hunting, fighting, and so
on). And the same goes for words and sentences, which are as
important in many ritual or magical practices as gestures are, in
incantations, spells, curses, in prayers, vows, and so on. There
may be words used only in ritual magic, but these are taken as
words with the power that words have in speech – conversation,
instructions, orders, quarrels, etc., outside ritual – a power
which they bring with them into ritual.

The words and gestures of daily speech. Otherwise they
would not be gestures or words. The ritual *means* something to
those who celebrate or take part in it. Depending on which rite
it is, there must be just these gestures, just these words must be
uttered, and they must come in this order. What is done and
spoken in the ritual refers to something important in the lives of
the people who practise it: to sunrise at the solstices or
equinoxes, to planting and harvesting, to the coming of the
rainy season, to birth, to marriage, to burial, to going into
battle, etc. It can do this, it has this significance because "it is the
same language" – the language in which they plan and go about
their sowing and harvesting, the language of their hopes and
fears regarding it. When Wittgenstein says that all the shifts
from one use of a symbol in a ritual to another or "figurative"
use of it are familiar or "natural" in our own ways of speaking,
he would assume they were natural also in the speech of those
people *outside* ritual.

What is it about the sequence of words and gestures which
shows that this is a ritual? If an anthropologist described the

daily life of one of the peoples Frazer mentions – what the men do, the sort of things the women do, the games the children play, and gave examples of the sort of questions they would ask and the sort of remarks they would make to one another in the course of this – we should not think he was telling us about some rite or ceremony. Why is it easy to recognize a rite when Frazer is describing it (even supposing we have opened the book so that we missed Frazer's remarks in introducing his account)? The *formal* character of a ritual is one of its marks. And this is important for Wittgenstein's discussion because, we might say, the repetition and keeping constantly to a strict form makes it plain that nobody is telling anyone anything or asking to be informed of anything in this use of language and of figures of speech. "[Here] we have . . . the use of an elaborate gesture-language." But the people are not using the gestures here as they do in talking together or in addressing a public meeting.

It is as though they assumed that the words and gestures had some powers in themselves: with words and gestures I can tell my neighbour something or deceive him; words also embody knowledge or wisdom, even in the presence of someone who cannot share it, just as words may contain a curse or a blessing. It is as though there might be a *performance* by words and gestures, in which the people who made and uttered them were stage hands or altar servants.

Wittgenstein mentions (p. 237) the ceremony of adopting a child, in which the mother draws the child through her clothes (see *The Golden Bough*, pp. 14, 15). This is like a figure of speech; something like a *description* of actual birth, although a symbolic and abbreviated one. It is a figure which *might* have been used to tell of an actual birth; but this is not how it is in the ceremony. She is not describing what has happened or trying to tell anyone what it is like.

4. A common source of confusion in philosophy, Wittgenstein thought, is to imagine the sense of meaning of a sentence as something which is "there" where the sentence is. "You look at

the sentence, and not at how it is used": for example, "The series of cardinal numbers is infinite" or Cantor's rule for his diagonal procedure.

About a year before these comments on Frazer, Wittgenstein wrote:

> It would be characteristic of a certain false conception of things if a philosopher were to believe that he had to have a proposition printed in red, because only so would it express the whole of what the author wanted to say. (This would be the magical instead of the logical conception of signs.)
>
> (A magical sign would work like a drug and in that case the causal theory would be quite satisfactory.) (MS 109, 89–90)

By "the causal theory" he means here 'the causal theory of meaning' which we find, for instance, in *The Meaning of Meaning* by C. K. Ogden and I. A. Richards (London, 1923) and in many writings of Bertrand Russell.

Wittgenstein writes of "the magical instead of the logical conception of signs". The logical view sees signs as belonging to a system or to a language. To see what the force or effectiveness of a sign is, look at the way(s) it is used in a game or language. I see the sign as magical when I take its efficacy to lie in these physical marks or sounds or movements.

Later, he wrote in the manuscript with the comments on Frazer:

> 'The way' I comply with the rule (if the word is to have any sense at all) must be what is expressed by a further rule. If there is no such further rule, there is no *way* of applying the first rule; there is simply its application. A way, here, would be as opposed to another way. (MS 110, 125)

5.   If someone "treats it as magical" in this sense, he shows

that he misunderstands what "being a symbol" or "having meaning" or "being language" is.

Wittgenstein spoke, in the *Tractatus* and elsewhere, of "misunderstanding the logic of our language". He said in the preface to the *Tractatus* that in its treatment of philosophical problems the book shows "that the reason why these problems are posed is that the logic of our language is misunderstood". He began the manuscript of these comments on Frazer by saying that the right way to begin his new book would be "with remarks on metaphysics as a form of magic" (p. 29). If he still held to what he said in the *Tractatus* preface, does this amount to saying that there is a kind of magic — the magic we can see in the writings and discussions on metaphysics — which is practised from a misunderstanding of the logic of language? This would not imply that this misunderstanding underlies *all* magic; or that it is present in "the ancient rituals".

Wittgenstein would not call an ancient ritual practice "metaphysics". But the misunderstanding of the logic of language (or of the way language functions) gives rise to metaphysics. This does not mean that metaphysical questions or theories are *about* language, that metaphysics puts forward a theory of language which is wrong. Nor does it say that a mis-understanding of the logic of language could lead to nothing else. And he might have said that the hold of ancient rituals on people also rested on such a misunderstanding.

It is hard to make clear the kind of "misunderstanding" this is, especially when we think it shows elsewhere than in philosophy. It is not like misunderstanding the theory of relativity or misunderstanding the role of heredity in the quality of crops or misunderstanding set theory. It cannot be explained except by illustrations and examples.

In *Philosophical Investigations*, I, §§92, 93, he is speaking of the inclination in philosophy to ask, "*What is* language?", "What is: *saying* something?": because the visible or audible signs don't

seem to be that by which we are guided when we read or listen
or give a proof.

93.   One person might say "A proposition is the most ordinary
thing in the world" and another: "A proposition – that's
something very queer" – And the latter is unable simply to look
and see how propositions really work. The forms that we use in
expressing ourselves about propositions and thought stand in his
way.

Why do we say that a proposition is something remarkable?
On the one hand because of the enormous importance attaching
to it. (And that is correct.) On the other hand this, together with
a misunderstanding of the logic of language, seduces us into
thinking that something extraordinary, something unique, must
be achieved by propositions. – A *misunderstanding* makes it look to
us as if a proposition *did* something queer.

"*Die Formen unserer Ausdrucksweise* . . ." The English translation has: "the forms that we use in expressing ourselves . . .". In
a typescript made soon after the manuscript of the comments on
Frazer, he made a short chapter of a few of them (and three
others of this time) which he headed: "The mythology in the
forms of our language ((Paul Ernst))." (The double parentheses
are a reminder to himself, I think, to acknowledge somewhere
in this context his indebtedness to Paul Ernst's epilogue to an
edition   of   the   Grimms'   *Märchen*   for   the   phrase
"misunderstanding the logic of language".)

In the manuscript (immediately after the paragraph ending
". . . 'object' and 'complex'", *The Human World*, p. 36) he
says that "the primitive forms of our language: substantive,
adjective and verb show the simple model, to whose form
language tends to bring everything" (". . . auf dessen Form sie
alles zu bringen sucht" (MS 110, 206)). This indicates something
like a tendency in language, a tendency the *Tractatus* had followed in giving the place it does to "the general form of proposition". But here, in the remark I have quoted, the emphasis is

on "Subject – Predicate". This can lead to many confusions of different sorts. One of the commonest comes in the way we take the phrase: *"talking about* something". Consider Russell's notation $(\exists x).fx$, for instance, and Wittgenstein's criticisms in *Philosophical Grammar*, pp. 202ff. and 265ff.

In a later manuscript, of 1945, he is writing of the phrase "I meant *him*":

I say, "Please come here", and beckon to him. I meant A and not B. I did mean him, there is no doubt about that. And yet it seems to be clear that unless I want to fabricate something there was no connection between me (or my speaking) and him other than, say, my glance and the like. This "meaning him" construed as a connection is like a myth. And a very powerful myth. Because whatever sort of connection I imagine none of them does what I want. No connection that I can imagine will be adequate, and consequently it seems that meaning must be a specific connection quite incomparable with all other forms of connection. (MS 116, 275)

With this compare the passage, from the same manuscript, which appears (with a slight revision) in *Philosophical Investigations*.

When you tell me that you cursed and meant N. as you did so it is all one to me whether you looked at a picture of him, or imagined him, uttered his name, or what. The conclusions from this fact that interest me have nothing to do with these things. On the other hand, however, someone might explain to me that cursing was *effective* only when one had a clear image of the man or spoke his name out loud. But we should not say "The point is how the man who is cursing *means* his victim." (§680)

And he adds: "Nor, of course, does one ask: 'Are you sure that you cursed *him*, that the connection with him was established?'" (§681)

In certain societies, uttering a curse on someone may be a terrible thing. In some this may depend upon the rank or the relationship of the person who utters it: if uttered by a priest or by one's father it might be terrible, but otherwise less so. When I say it is terrible I refer to the role it would have in that society; to a host of institutions, beliefs, and practices which enter when I think of how a curse is taken up and regarded there; to notions of honour and of dignity among the members; to the relations of the victim and his family, and to what he may feel called upon to do now, etc. The "effectiveness" of the curse will depend on the circumstances or the culture in which it is uttered. Generally, I suppose, there is no doubt who is meant. And *this* – who is meant – is determined by various things the person uttering it says or does, perhaps by his relation to the victim before and afterwards. If he tells us that he had a clear image of the victim as he was pronouncing it, all right; but this does no more to establish a connection of the curse with the victim than the relevant words and actions do.

It may have been important to *me* that I had a clear image of him in mind and spoke my curse to it (almost as if I had been spitting at his picture). But the image did not fix who it was or what it was I was talking about, any more clearly than did the words I was using. The present author made a note of the following remark at a lecture delivered in 1936: "For the CONNECTION is made in applying what we say – it is not something which is given all at once." To say "Unless I have a mental image of him at the time, the curse will not be effective" is like saying ". . . otherwise the curse will not really be a curse." It is not ". . . otherwise it will not be a curse on *him*" (as though, if I did not have the image, I could not be cursing anyone in particular), nor is it "if I am to mean him in my curse, I must mean him in this way." This would not be the ordinary use of "mean". In our everyday talking and writing and reading it would make sense to ask, "Did you mean *him*?", but not, "*How* did you mean him?"; as though you might answer, "I meant him in *this* way – as opposed to that way or that other way." You might have used that sentence if the word were ambiguous, as you might explain, "I was using 'board' in the sense of Coal Board, not of floor board.' But this is not what the person is trying to say who speaks of "*how* you mean him when you pronounce the curse".

When someone says this, he is trying to use the expression in an *invented* application (*"eine erfundene Anwendung"*), although he does not realize or admit that it *is* invented.

I want the utterance of the curse to be something like *hitting* him. If I hit him, there is a 'connection'; and that is the sort of connection that is important for me. But uttering the words and having or drawing the image can be *something like* hitting him only because they are words and symbols understood in the syntax of ordinary language; which establishes the 'connection' both with him and with hitting.

In such a case Wittgenstein says "the invented use, or application" is like a myth: "This 'meaning him' construed as a connection is like a myth." We cannot describe it by anything it has in common with other uses of language, and we cannot correct it as you might correct or point out to me in the ordinary way my misunderstanding of the grammar of some expression I was using. And if I take "meaning him" as a connection of my words with him, this illustrates what "misunderstanding of the logic of language" is.

When Wittgenstein says "a very *powerful* mythology" (*"ein sehr starker Mythos"*), he means the powerful hold it has on the man's thinking. Perhaps he also means that it is hard to keep from falling into this way of viewing "what it is that makes speaking of him *speaking of HIM*": that the tendency in our language towards this way of thinking must be very strong. Wittgenstein sometimes speaks of *"eine* Verhexung *durch die* Sprache (*durch die* Formen *der Sprache)"* (*"a bewitchment* by language (by the *forms* of language)", or of *"eine* Verstrickung" (*"an entanglement"*), from which it is astonishingly difficult to free oneself. It is an obstacle to that understanding, to that *"Einsicht in das Arbeiten unserer Sprache"*, which is the work of philosophy. The passage in *Philosophical Investigations* runs:

> These philosophical problems are, of course, not empirical problems; they are solved, rather, by looking into the workings of our language, and that in such a way as to make us recognize those workings: *in despite of* an urge to misunderstand them. (§109)

(The English translation renders *"durch eine Einsicht in das Arbeiten unserer Sprache"* as: "by looking into the workings of our language". I doubt if this can be bettered. But it might suggest to a new reader something like looking into the workings of the organs of a body in physiology. "Insight" could mislead in the other way; but there *is* something of this here. Wittgenstein commonly drew his parallels from "difficulties" in mathematics and in aesthetics.)

In the next remark of *Philosophical Investigations* he gives an example of this "bewitchment of our understanding": "Language (or thought) is something unique" – this proves to be a superstition (*not* a mistake!), itself produced by grammatical illusions." (§110) *Aberglaube* – superstition – is not a mistake. But it shows a want of understanding (it is "produced by grammatical illusions") and in this sense it is a *fault* (*ein Tadel*).

Frazer seemed to think that the people who practised the rites he mentions were making a *mistake*: they were trying to follow natural happenings or control them, but their theories were wrong. Wittgenstein thought this was a misunderstanding:

> There is a mistake only if magic is presented as science. (p. 31)
> What makes the character of ritual action is not any view or opinion, either right or wrong. . . . (p. 33)

"So Wittgenstein was coming forward in defence of the

ancient rituals!" That remark could have sense only if Wittgenstein had recognized no other "coordinates", no other standards than that of knowledge, of what may be established in science, and error; (and probably it would not have sense even then).

6. Some months before he began the first comments on Frazer, Wittgenstein wrote of the scapegoat ritual:

> The scapegoat, on which sins are laid and which goes out into the wilderness with them, is a false picture, like all the false pictures of philosophy. Philosophy might be said to purify thought from a misleading mythology. (MS 109, 210f.)

"A false picture, or a misleading picture." Sometimes we could say 'analogy' instead of 'picture'. When Wittgenstein writing the comments on Frazer — he turned aside to write on other topics fairly often — he said:

> Whenever I put right a philosophical error, saying that things have always been pictured in a certain way but are not really so, I always have to point out some analogy that has governed thinking but has not been recognized as an analogy. (MS 110, 193)

". . . I must always show an analogy in which he has thought, although he has not seen it as analogy."

In the rite of the scapegoat (Leviticus 16:20—22) several analogies come together. It would be natural in a tribal society to speak of "bearing the sins of others": of a family sharing the sin committed by any member of it, or of children bearing the sins of their forefathers. The sins of the people come between them and God. But purification was possible through sacrifice, and then the people could turn to God again for help. Here there are metaphors enough, but they need not mislead anyone. Suppose then: "If the people assembled here do bear the sins of their fathers, and of their brothers now living, then why should not the priest bring in some animal to be made one of them in this sense only – that it bears their sins – and then, after laying his hands on it, send it with their sins away from them into the wilderness?" When Wittgenstein calls this rite a misleading picture, he may mean something like this: consider

1 "Children carry the sins of their fathers."

2 "A goat, when consecrated, carries the sins of the people." In the first sentence "carry" is used in the sense of the whole sentence. In the second sentence "carry" seems to mean what it does in "The goat carries on his back the basket in which we put our firewood"; and yet it *cannot* mean that.

Of course a living animal may be taken as a symbol together with the other symbols, the symbolic performance, in the ritual. But in this case Wittgenstein thought the symbol, in the role that was given it, was badly misleading.

(If we called it an *incongruous* simile, we should be speaking in a different tongue and a different culture; we should be saying how the account of this strikes us now. Perhaps we should not find it incongruous – we should not find the picture jars in symbolizing what is intended for it – if you said that a *man* might take on himself the sins the people have had to bear, and offer himself in atonement for them. But a goat? What would it mean to say that a goat has to bear its *own* sins, let alone that it has to bear the sins of *people*? Bunyan's image of Christian bearing his sins like a heavy pack on his shoulders does not jar in this way. I am bewildered by the separate roles of the two goats in the rituals described in Leviticus. The goat that takes on itself the sins of the people is not killed and sacrificed in an offering to God. The people may have looked on the goat that was slaughtered as something they offered in place of their first born – as Abraham saw the ram that God told him to offer in place of his son. But it is hard to see the substitution in the scapegoat that delivers them of their sins. I do not know how they thought of this. Nor does anyone now. This does not affect the point Wittgenstein is making.)

Wittgenstein says in the practice of magic – and so in much of ritual – there is the portrayal of a wish. Just before this is the sentence: "The portrayal of a wish is, eo ipso, the portrayal of its fulfilment" (*The Human World*, p. 31, though there "*Darstellung*" is translated as "description"). Here the word "fulfilment" ("*Erfüllung*") gives trouble. Wittgenstein was writing on this while he was writing these comments on Frazer. But if we leave this on one side a moment, many would feel that "the magic in a ritual gives expression to a wish – it is a portrayal of a wish" has something in it; although we want to add that it is unlike the expression of a wish in everyday life. In much that we call ritual or magic, the words and the movements and the chants come in a prescribed order, like steps in a liturgy. If I tell my friend what I wish, or if I tell a public meeting, it is not like this. A more serious trouble shows when we ask about "portrayal" ("*Darstellung*"), or "symbolizing".

We may think first that the picture set out in the scapegoat ritual is a form of symbolism of form of expression: the way in which those people expressed their longing for release from the burden of sin. But suppose someone asked, "Do they *get* the purification for which they have longed, when the scapegoat is sent into the wilderness?" Would this be all a misunderstanding? Or is there not something that does make us want to ask it?

It would show misunderstanding if we meant that these people thought that by expressing their wish in this way they could secure the fulfilment (the removal of their sins) as a *consequence* of going through these motions. The question is more like asking: "Is the performance of the ritual itself the experience of purification? Is what they long for taking place in this portrayal of it?" If we say it is, then are we not saying that the scapegoat shows a confusion of what belongs to the symbolism or phraseology with what is portrayed or described in this phraseology? We might call this confusion a more fundamental misunderstanding of the logic of language than we find, say, in the misunderstanding of the functioning or the grammar of "mean" in "When I said 'Come here' I meant A and not B". (Although, if we do say this we have not thought far enough. Compare: "'That's meant to be *him*' (this picture represents *him*) – that contains the whole problem of representation" (own translation, *Philosophical Grammar*, p. 102).

7. There is a tendency to confuse what belongs to the symbolism with what is expressed in that symbolism – especially in expression of a wish, or of an expectation or an intention. Wittgenstein was writing about expectation, wish, intention, in the beginning of 1930 and he often returned to it. He sometimes wrote as though 'expectation' were the general term and much that he said of it would hold for wishing and for intention as well; but then he would speak of wishing and of intention specially – of important points in which their grammars were different.

In *Philosophical Remarks* the discussion of expectation begins on page 57:

What does it mean to say 'Admittedly I can't see any red, but if you give me a paint-box, I can point it out to you'? How can you *know* that you will be able to point it out if . . .; and so, that you will be able to recognize it when you see it?

This might mean two different kinds of things: it might express the expectation that I shall recognize it if I am shown it, in the same sense that I expect a headache if I'm hit on the head; then it is, so to speak, an expectation that belongs to physics, with the same sort of grounds as any other expectation relating to the occurrence of a physical event. – Or else it has nothing to do with expecting a physical event, and for that reason neither would my proposition be falsified if such an event should fail to occur. Instead, it's as if the proposition is saying that I possess a paradigm that I could at any time compare the colour with. (And the 'could' here is logical possibility.) (§11)

If I expect an event and that which fulfils my expectation occurs, does it then make sense to ask whether that really is the event I expected? i.e. how would a proposition that asserted this be verified? It is clear that the *only* source of knowledge I have here is a comparison of the *expression* of my expectation with the event that has occurred. (p. 65, §25)

... For expecting that *p* will be the case must be the same as expecting that this expectation will be fulfilled; ... (p. 65, §25)

The event which takes the place of an expectation, answers it: i.e. the replacement constitutes the answer, so that no question can arise whether it really is the answer. Such a question would mean putting the *sense* of a proposition in question. (p. 68, §29)

These remarks would hold (with verbal adjustments in the first two) of 'wishing' as of 'expecting'.

While he was writing these comments on Frazer — or rather, at intervals in his writing them — he wrote in the same manuscript on the distinction between "the bearer of a name" and "the·meaning of a name", and he wrote also those remarks on "complex" and "fact" ("Komplex ≠ Tatsache") which are now in *Philosophical Grammar* (pp. 199–201). In the manuscript his discussion of "complex and fact" grows out of and continues a discussion of: "We can never describe anything except in general terms".

Whenever I talk about the fulfilment of a proposition, I talk about it in general. My description of it falls under some form or other. Indeed this generality is implicit in the fact that I can give the description in advance and certainly independently of the occurrence of the fact.

(These propositions are indicative of severe grammatical disorders.)

When I say, "I talk about the fulfilment of a proposition *in general*", I mean that I talk in words that are not produced specially for this occasion.

When we say that the fact is described in "a general way", we contrast this mentally with some other way. (But of course we derive this contrast from somewhere else.) We imagine that the fulfilment consists in something new coming into existence which was not there before. We imagine, that is, an object or complex that we can now point to, or that can put itself forward, whereas the description was only a picture of it. As if I had painted in advance the apple that was going to grow on this branch and now here it is itself. It might then be said that the description of the apple was general – i.e. effected by means of words and pigments etc., which existed before the apple did and not specially for its sake. A load of junk, as it were, in comparison with the real apple. Prefigurations that all have to abdicate when the thing expected itself arrives.

The fulfilment consists, though, not in the thing expected but in the fact *that* it has arrived.

This mistake is anchored deep within our language. We say, "I am expecting him", "I am awaiting his arrival", and "I expect that he will come".

Giving a general description of a fact means constructing it out of old components.

We describe *it*, the fact, exactly as if it was given to us not only by the description but in some other way also.

Here the fact is put on the same footing as a house or some similar complex.

An hypothesis can be construed in such a way that it does not go beyond experience, i.e. is not the expression of an expectation of future experience. Thus the proposition "There seems to be a lamp on the table in front of me" *can* do no more than describe my experience (or, as is usually said, my immediate experience).

What about the accuracy of such descriptions? Is it true to say, My visual picture is so complicated that it is impossible to describe it in full? This is a very fundamental question.

One seems to be saying that something is indescribable or not describable with the means currently available – or that one does not know how to describe it. (Questions, or problems, in mathematics.)

How then is *it* given to one – I mean the thing one does not know how to describe? – My visual picture is after all not a painted picture, nor is it the slice of nature that I see, in which case I could investigate it more closely. – Is *it* – this thing – already articulated and the only difficulty that of representing it in words? Or is it still in need of articulation?

"The flower was of a reddish-yellow colour, which however I cannot describe more accurately (or cannot describe in words more accurately)" – what does this mean?

"I can see it before my eyes and could paint it."

When one says one cannot accurately describe a particular colour in words, one is thinking of the possibility of such a description (naturally, otherwise the expression "accurate description" would have no sense): one has in mind the case in which a measurement was not carried out because the instruments were not accurate enough. (MS 110, 247–9 & 258–9)

"I can give only a general description" – this seems to allude to some description which I cannot give: to some way in which I cannot describe it. But then I cannot compare it with what I do say. And I could not tell you that any description which I do give is inadequate by comparison with that one. You can say my description is inadequate and suggest a better one. But you cannot suggest a description in words whose meanings cannot be explained in general terms, so that they cannot be used in other contexts, describing other situations.

This shows "a grave illness in the functioning of the grammar through which these expressions are intelligible": how in the normal following of this grammar, and *from* the normal functioning, we think we are contemplating an expression like 'fulfilment' and we find in it questions which seem to make *any* expression in language unintelligible. "This mistake is anchored deep within our language." If I wish my brother would come to see me, then it is not my brother that will fulfil my wish, but *that he has come*. Wittgenstein is emphasizing the superficial parallel between "the coming of my brother" and "the coming of an event". Confusions may come from this, obviously. But Wittgenstein would not have said there need be anything mistaken in our using the different forms of expression: "I am expecting him", "I am expecting him to come", and "I expect that he will come". He would not have said that only the second of these expresses correctly what the fulfilment of my expectation would be. If you asked "What are you waiting for?" and I answered "I'm waiting for my brother", there would be nothing inaccurate or inadequate in this; and Wittgenstein would not have said, "what you *really* mean is you are waiting for your brother to come."

Whoever said it would be confusing the meaning of a name and the bearer of a name. Or at any rate, he would be unclear in some way about this distinction. If we tried to think of the bearer of a name without bringing in any of the "content" of the name by which we distinguish him (or it), we should not be speaking of anything. In the same passage, just after what I have quoted, there appears in parenthesis: "'I am looking for him.' – 'What does he look like?' – 'I don't know, but I'll recognize him when I see him.'" (MS 110, 276) And there may be a similar confusion about the meanings of colour words (or the words of shapes or movements, such as 'turning', 'jumping', etc.). In a manuscript six months earlier Wittgenstein wrote,

We confuse the word "green" with the proposition "a is green". (Hence too our difficulty to define it in the proposition "a is not green".). . . . I.e. we think that the word itself contains what in fact finds expression only in the proposition. (MS 109, 213)

When we distinguish 'the meaning of a name' and 'the bearer of the name' we recognize a distinction in grammar. In other words, we explain the distinction by mentioning statements and questions that could be made and asked about the bearer of the name and could not be made or asked about the meaning of the name – where the "could not" is a logical or grammatical one.

> How odd! I can look for him when he is not there, but I cannot point at him when he is not there. That is the real problem of "looking for" and shows the misleadingness of the comparison.
> One might be tempted to say, But he must actually be there if I am looking for him. – Then he must also be there if I do not find him, and also if he does not exist. (MS 110, 274)

Fifteen manuscript pages later (in the manuscript which has the comments on Frazer):

> "I can imagine how that will be." (When the chair has been painted white.) But how can I imagine it, when it hasn't been?! Is imagination a kind of sorcery? No: the description of what one imagines is not the same as the description of the expected occurrence. (MS 110, 289)

We might expect him then to revise his earlier remark: "The portrayal of a wish is eo ipso the portrayal of its fulfilment." "*Darstellung*" ("portrayal") is not just the same as "*Beschreibung*" ("description"); in *Philosophical Remarks*, for example Wittgenstein says: "A form cannot be described: it can only be presented (*dargestellt*)." (p. 208) But after he had written ". . . is, eo ipso, the portrayal of its fulfilment" he wrote the remarks on "complex and fact" (see *Philosophical Remarks*, pp. 301–303; *Philosophical Grammar*, pp. 199–201). And I wonder if the phrase, "*die* Darstellung *seiner Erfüllung*", ("the *portrayal* of its fulfilment"), would be appropriate in the light of what he says in them; for example:

> Now, you can, of course, point at a constellation and say: this

constellation is composed entirely of objects with which I am already acquainted; but you can't 'point at a fact' and say this. . . .

To point out (*hinweisen auf*) a fact means to assert something, to state something. 'To point at' (*hinweisen auf*) a flower doesn't mean this.

A chain too is composed of its links, not of these and their spatial relations.

The fact that these links are so concatenated isn't '*composed*' of anything at all.

The root of this muddle is the confusing use of the word 'object'.

If I translate "*Darstellung*" roughly in the phrases: "portrayal of my wish . . . portrayal of that which would satisfy my wish", then this second phrase is not the same as, "portraying the *satisfaction* of my wish" or "portraying the arrival of what I wish for".

In *Philosophical Remarks* Wittgenstein had said:

. . . you cannot describe an expectation unless you can give a description *comparing* the expectation with the present, of the form: *Now* I see a red circle *here*, and expect a blue square *there later on*.

That is to say the yardstick of language must be applied at the point which is present and then points out beyond it – roughly speaking, in the direction of the expectation. (p. 72)

About two years later he wrote in a pencilled amendment to his typescript:

I want to say that in order to determine the place of the thing wished for my proposition must be placed upon the present situation like a ruler pointing in a certain direction. How else would it indicate the point in space where the thing wished for is meant to be? But even when the ruler is so positioned against reality, why must I then interpret it as just this wish? The difficulty we are here trying to resolve is once again this: How does the wish determine the thing wished for? And we are once again vainly trying to anticipate the fulfilment of the wish in the wish itself. (MS 213, 389)

(Compare: "How does a proposition determine the fact that validates it?")

When he goes on from "The description (*Darstellung*) of a wish . . ." to "And magic does give representation (*Darstellung*) to a wish . . ." (*The Human World*, p. 31) he would have to say that the *interpretation* of this "portrayal" (*Darstellung*) is still open. If the ritual of the scapegoat is the portrayal of a wish, what do we mean when we say that the symbolism is inappropriate or misleading? Among different peoples, substituting animals for men as victims for sacrifice seems to have taken different forms – different animals were used, and perhaps the significance the offered animal had for them, the way they read the substitution, differed from one people to another. Granted that there is something like a move in our verbal language – a shift in the way a symbol is used, and so in what is symbolized – we cannot say what this is in a particular case (say the symbol of the scapegoat) unless we know the people who celebrate this ritual: unless we know how their language and their use of images is interwoven with the other activities in their lives. We do not know in what sense it should be seen as acting out the fulfilment of a wish.

Wittgenstein also said: "The ritual of the ancient myths was a language." I find this wonderfully illuminating; yet I do not grasp it distinctly enough to give examples that would illustrate it. The ritual brings or gives expression to the *myths* which there are in the lives of those people. I am reminded of the suggestion that a church (a small Norman church or a Gothic cathedral) may "give visible form to" religious ideas. And the sense in

which we might say of the architecture or of the ritual that it is
"a language" – this analogy might be developed. Differences
are plain enough. But it hints at the direction in which we might
think of ritual ("*der Ritus der alten Mythen*") as "a language". –
Repetition and performance is not in the architecture, but it is at
the heart of ritual. Repetition and performance of music is not
the same, except where the music is part of a ritual. If we said
"the ritual gives expression to a myth" we should have come
closer than we do in "the ritual gives expression to a wish".

When Wittgenstein speaks of "myth" in discussing philosophy, there is a suggestion of something akin to a wish.
He speaks here of a *tendency* in our language and our thinking; of
the strong *attraction*, like a myth, which holds us to some mis-
conception of the grammar of some expression; of the *impulse*
which resists the investigations which would remove it. But we
do not think of the fulfilment of a myth, as we do of a wish.

Would he have said the ritual of the ancient myth was a
practice which resists or stands in the way of clarification? Not
always. But it might be. And perhaps at this time (1930) he
would have thought it most likely.

B

In the 1930 draft of his preface (his final version is printed as
the foreword to *Philosophical Remarks*) Wittgenstein wrote:

> The danger of a long preface is that it ought to make manifest the
> spirit of the book and this cannot be described. . . .

> But it is true to say that, in my opinion, this book has nothing
> to do with the progressive civilization of Europe and America –
> that this civilization is perhaps the environment essential to the
> spirit of the book, but that the two have different goals.

> Everything ritual (everything high-priestly, as it were) must
> be strictly avoided, because it immediately turns bad. A kiss, to be
> sure, is also a ritual, and does not go bad – but the only allowable
> ritual is what is as genuine as a kiss.

It is a great temptation, to try to make the spirit of something explicit. (MS 109, 208–9)

Most ritual acts and utterances corrupt or contaminate what they present. If Wittgenstein's book were offered to the public in an introduction that degraded the spirit in which it had been written, this would obstruct the sort of clarification that his discussions might have brought – even though the reader understood those discussions in the sense of being able to follow what was said in them, to see that one remark bears on what is said in another, and so on. In the same set of drafts for his preface he says: "Whether the typical western scientist will understand or appreciate me is a matter of indifference to me, because, after all, he does not understand the spirit in which I write." (MS 109, 206) We may say, perhaps, that then the reader misunderstands what is written. This is not the same as '*failing* to understand' when someone cannot follow the paragraphs or finds them utterly obscure. In the second set of comments on the *Golden Bough*, Wittgenstein might have said that Frazer does not understand the spirit, the *Geist*, of the fire-festivals and of human sacrifice; in this sense he does not understand what they are, although he can give detailed accounts of them, knows when and where they were practised, and can say with high probability what the practices were from which these now on record were descended.

About the time of the earlier comments on Frazer Wittgenstein tried to show and perhaps to formulate the difference between 'misunderstanding' and 'not understanding'. ('*Missverständnis*' – '*Unverständnis*'). On one page he wrote: "Here (on this page) I wanted to display the essence of misunderstanding language, as opposed to not understanding it." (MS 213, 35) Where he spoke of a "*mis*understanding of the logic of language", obviously he did not mean that when I fall into this misunderstanding I show that I do not know the language. It is only because I understand the grammar of words like 'cause' and 'thinking' – only then is it possible (logically possible) to misunderstand them when I reflect on what a cause must be or what thinking must be. When you correct my grammar you show that I am ignorant of it at some point; this is not like showing that I have misunderstood the grammar I know. It would be more natural to say I had *not* understood the spirit in which the book is written. And he says I have *mis*understood, this is not like misunderstanding the logic or the functioning of language.

"Everything ritual (everything high-priestly, as it were) . . ." The sense of this may be clearer from what he says in the printed preface: "I should like to say, 'This book is written to the glory of God', but nowadays that would be chicanery, that is, it would not be rightly understood." (*Philosophical Remarks*, foreword) The English translation has "chicanery . . .", but "*eine Schurkerei*" is much stronger than that. Mr John Stonborough called my attention to this. "The trick of a blackguard" would come nearer, except that "blackguard" is not just common-or-garden English any more. Wittgenstein does not suggest that the expression "written to the glory of God" would at all times have had something 'high-priestly' about it. It did not when Bach wrote it on the title-page of his manuscript, and Bach had no reason to think it would not be understood as it was meant.

But the expression would not have been so understood if Wittgenstein had written it on his title-page in 1930. This would have been one form of misunderstanding (*Missverständnis*). It would not in itself be a misunderstanding of the spirit of the book. But it would make that understanding difficult and unlikely. The "*Schurkerei*" it showed would be incompatible with the spirit in which Wittgenstein's book was written. Which does not mean that it would be incompatible with anything said or written in the book. The incompatibility with the *Geist* or spirit of the book would show in other ways. Two days before he wrote this draft of the preface, he wrote in the manuscript book a comment on a passage from Renan's *Peuple d'Israel*, and in the course of it:

> . . . it is wrong to say, Of course, all phenomena *were bound* to leave primitive peoples open-mouthed. But perhaps everything in their environment *did* leave these peoples open-mouthed. – That they were bound to be open-mouthed is a primitive superstition. (Like the belief that they were bound to be afraid of all the forces of nature.) But experience may perhaps show that certain primitive tribes are very liable to be afraid of natural phenomena. – It is not excluded, however, that highly civilized races may once again be liable to this same fear; and their civilization and scientific knowledge will not protect them from it. To be sure, it is true that the *spirit* in which science is conducted nowadays could not be combined with such a fear. (MS 109, 101–2)

I have quoted this solely for the phrase: "that the *spirit* in which science is conducted nowadays could not be combined with such a fear".

Anything in the preface to his book that smelt of ritual or the utterances of a high priest "could not be combined with the spirit of the book", would be incompatible with its having been written in good will (and not out of vanity or self-assertiveness).

The same words and sentences might have been written in a different spirit – just as the book might be read aloud in a different spirit (so as to make a kind of paraody of it) – and then the talent in the book might come through as more scornful and envious and perhaps hypocritical than a work of mediocre talent could be. "A kiss, to be sure, is also a ritual, and does not go bad – but the only allowable ritual is what is as genuine as a kiss." The *Fäulnis*, the corruption, that ritual generally shows, is that it is not *echt*. It is like trying to be something that one is not. When he was writing about 'taste' in connection with aesthetics, Wittgenstein said, "Taste makes things *acceptable*". He might have said this of a kiss, and also of a preface that was as straightforward and genuine as a kiss. "This preface makes the book acceptable." A kiss may be false. In his comments on the fire-festivals (to which I shall refer) he says that the practice of using bits of cake for casting lots to determine who is to be the sacrificial victim strikes us as particularly terrible, "almost like betrayal by a kiss". The form of that betrayal was terrible because a kiss is unambiguous.

I have said that the expression 'incompatible with the spirit of the book' is not the same as 'incompatible with some statement or some paragraph or some conclusion drawn in the book', and I suggested that what is said or printed in the book, in this sense, might have been written there in a different spirit from that in which Wittgenstein wrote it. At any rate, we can imagine different ways in which the book might be read aloud. Wittgenstein also spoke of the *spirit* of the mainstream of European and American civilization in which we all are. He might have spoken of the spirit of a particular tribe or people during a particular period in its history; I am not sure.

The senses of the expressions 'spirit' and 'myth' may partly coalesce in special contexts. Obviously they are not the same throughout. If someone should speak of the myths that belong to the life of this tribe or people, we should think, perhaps, of traditional stories of the origin of their race, of the origin of their form of worship, the origin of their laws, and so on. The myths may express a way of looking on their existence as a people. But the telling of the myths and the spirit in which the people enter into them or hold to them may change with time. I say "hold to them", and I might have said "believe them". If we tried to explain what 'believe them' would mean here, we should see that it might mean to say that the belief has not the same form, or that the way it shows in their way of living is different now from what it was earlier. In a later manuscript (of 1945) Wittgenstein wrote:

We are told that primitive tribes believe they are descended from an animal – e.g. from a snake. We wonder, How can they believe that? We ought to ask, How *do* they believe it? They perhaps utter words which we translate into the English sentence "We are descended from . . ." But, one immediately says, that is not all, they have the most manifold practices and laws, all based on this belief (which therefore show that we have made a *correct* translation of their words into English! But why should we not say, These customs and laws are not *based* on the belief: they show *to what extent* (in what sense) such a belief exists.

One might ask for example, Do the people in question ever believe, in everyday life, that a snake gives birth to a human being rather than to a snake? "According as this question is answered in one way or in another, their belief has from its origin a different field."

Suppose a race calls itself "the children of Israel". Originally, I suppose, that did not mean the descendants of a man called Israel. No, "descendants" or "children" meant the same as the "tribe", viewed as a temporal phenomenon. As if the development of π was called "the children of π".

Now suppose that 'by a misunderstanding' the expression was interpreted as the children or descendants of one Israel, so that there was talk of a man Israel who was their ancestor: the question is, In what sort of cases is it right to talk of a misunderstanding, and in what cases just of a figure of speech? Prima facie, we should expect all sorts and degrees. And that, in certain religions, what was originally a figure of speech would exuberate into full misunderstanding. (Perhaps with the help of philosophers.) (MS 116, 283–5)

PART II

1. The longest and most interesting of Wittgenstein's later set of comments are on the descriptions of the Beltane fire-festival (May fire) as it was performed by children in eighteenth-century Scotland. Frazer quotes fairly full descriptions from three writers who lived or travelled in Scotland in the latter half

of the eighteenth century. This comes in his chapter on "The
Fire-Festivals in Europe", which tells of festivals in France,
Germany, Austria, Switzerland, Bulgaria, Hungary, Russia,
Lithuania, Esthonia, etc. These are all fire-festivals – in this
they are all alike. But granting this, Wittgenstein says then the
most remarkable thing is the extent of the *differences* one from
another.

> It is a wide variety of faces with common features. . . . And one
> would like to draw lines joining the parts that various faces have
> in common. But then a part of our contemplation would still be
> lacking, and it is what connects this picture with our own feelings
> and thoughts. This part gives the contemplation its depth.

He adds:

> In all these practices we see something that is similar at any rate,
> to the association of ideas and related to it. We could speak of an
> association of practices. (*The Human World*, p. 37)

"In all these practices we see something. . . ." Wittgenstein's
comments are centred on this "something", on bringing out
what this is, or perhaps better, on clarifying "*seeing* something
in all these practices".

For it is not something we can *see*, in the sense in which we
can see the features in the faces of different portrait-photographs
and draw lines connecting them when the photographs are
placed together in an album. Whatever it is, Wittgenstein says
here clearly it is not that.

2. Frazer and others offer theories of the origins of these
practices; and explain their origin by considering what "advan-
tages" the ancient people expected to gain from them (cf. *The
Golden Bough*, p. 652, §2). For Wittgenstein, this does not
explain what we express in calling any of them a ritual sacrifice.
Nor does it explain the disquieting impression which they leave

when we read of them. We feel in some way involved, in this impression, as we should not feel in reading the history of some piece of technology – say the development of the rudder in sailing ships. There is an impression of something deep and sinister, in the celebration of the Beltane festival by Scottish children 150 years ago, an impression that is the more disquieting when we are not clear why it strikes us, what it is about their celebration of May Day that strikes us so differently from anything we should find in an account of children's games of highwaymen in which they pretend to shoot or hang one another. It is queer that children should make a festivity out of going through the motions of burning a living man.

If we say with Frazer that in all probability this Beltane festival was a survival from an ancient ritual of human sacrifice, then in one sense we have explained it; explained, perhaps, the performance of it in this place and at this time of year, and also the burning of the straw figure. But in a sense that is more important for Wittgenstein, it *does not* explain. This shows in the disquieting impression we get from this festival as strongly after we have accepted the theory of its origin as before.

It would make no difference if the hypothesis, that human sacrifice was actually practised here at one time, turned out to be wrong. What is important is the multitude of considerations of the sort of 'game' it is (making a festival out of playing at burning a human being alive) and of the 'evidence' which makes its connection with an actual practice of human sacrifice overwhelmingly probable *prior* to any historical research and independently of anything the research may bring to light. The 'evidence' that is most important here is also what makes deep and sinister the thought of the actual human sacrifice in earlier times. It is evidence, we may say, part of which is not directly connected with the accounts of the Beltane festival nor with the actual human sacrifice as we may imagine it.

The disquieting impression when we think of the ritual sacrifice of a human being, as it was practised at one time, is

hardly different from, nor more disquieting than, the impression
we have from those descriptions of the children's celebration of
the Beltane fire-festival. And if the problem was to understand
the source of this impression, then we have simply pushed the
problem further back. We ask now why we feel something
deep and sinister in the ritual sacrifice of a human being.

> What makes human sacrifice something deep and sinister
> anyway? Is it only the suffering of the victim that impresses us in
> this way? All manner of diseases bring just as much suffering and
> do *not* make this impression. No, this deep and sinister aspect is
> not obvious just from learning the history of the external action,
> but *we* impute it from an experience in ourselves. (*The Human
> World*, p. 40)

But the meaning of this is not quite clear until we have looked at
more of what Wittgenstein says about what we "see" in those
descriptions of the Beltane festivals. In particular:

> Can I not feel horror from the thought that the cake with the
> knobs once served to select by lot the victim to be sacrificed?
> Hasn't the *thought* something terrible? – Yes, but that which I see
> in those stories is something they acquire, after all, from the
> evidence, including such evidence as does not seem directly con-
> nected with them – from the thought of man and his past, from
> the strangeness of what I see in myself and in others, what I have
> seen and have heard.

Notice here: "that which I *see* in those stories", "from the
strangeness of what I see in myself and in others . . .", and also
"is not obvious just from learning the history of the *external*
action".

3. Wittgenstein had spoken of what it is that brings us to
look on the variety of fire-festivals in a way that connects them
with our own feelings and thoughts. And he said it is this that
gives depth to what we say and think about them.

In almost the next comment, speaking of the Scottish minister's account of drawing the bits of cake from a bonnet as lots to choose "the *devoted* person" and his remark, "There is little doubt of these inhuman sacrifices having once been offered in this country . . ." (*The Golden Bough*, p. 619), Wittgenstein says:

Here it seems as though it were the hypothesis that gave the matter depth . . . what gives this practice depth is its *connection* with the burning of a man.

The way we look on these practices gives their connection with our thoughts. When the hypothesis strikes us as plausible or very probable, we think of the Beltane festival in its connection with the sacrifice of a human being by burning him. This is the setting or context in which we see or think of it. (This is part of what we mean by 'the impression' we have when we read or think of it.)

But "it gets its depth from the hypothesis" is misleading, since it suggests that the impression of depth will be justified or shown to be illusory by the results of the historical inquiry. And its 'connection with some ancient ritual sacrifice' would be an "*external*" connection. This would not belong to the way in which we think of the festival, or to the concept which forms our thinking of it. And 'concept' goes here with 'possibilities', in the sense of Wittgenstein's remark: "What is true and interesting is not to say this derives from that, but this could have been derived in that way" (*Synthese*, 17, p. 252 [not translated in *The Human World*]). It is similar with the remark which begins: "Here something looks like the ruins of a casting of lots. And through this aspect it suddenly gains depth." (*The Human World*, p. 39) When Wittgenstein speaks of "aspect" we think (or I do) of *Philosophical Investigations* II, xi, with the discussion of his examples in which 'seeing' and 'thinking' run together, not as components of a complex have to be thought of together, but as concepts may 'run together', and what we should *mean* by "seeing" is also what we should mean by "thinking" here.

> Hence the flashing (*Aufleuchten*) of an aspect on us seems half visual experience, half thought. (p. 197e)

> . . . but what I perceive in the dawning (*Aufleuchten*) of an aspect is not a property of the object, but an internal relation between it and other objects. (p. 212e)

(These go with other sorts of examples there, but they hardly need touching to make them fit our case.)

The notion of *Tiefe* (depth) here is akin to that in an earlier manuscript: "A proposition, when I understand it, acquires depth for me." Partly this is the difference between a sentence on the page when I do not understand it and the way in which it shows connections with other things I have said and heard, the way it suggests questions, etc., when I do (as though what is printed on the page were only an index). More important, probably, "It now engages with my life." A cogwheel meshes with others in a mechanism, I give it a kind of attention I did not give to the printed signs on the page before I understood them, it may change the way I look at something else, etc.

But there is more, which this analogy ("A proposition, when I understand it . . .") does not bring out. "This practice is obviously age-old." If we asked "How can anyone know this?" we should come back to the character of the festival itself. If

> I see a ruin and say: that must have been a house once, for nobody would construct a heap out of hewn and irregular stones like this. And if someone asked, how do you know that? I could only say: from my experience of people.

If what the children are performing here is obviously age-old, this gives it a depth. It would be different if we were told that these children just took to doing this, on their own invention, because of some recent happening that had never been known before. When we think of what they do as something their fathers observed and practised every year at this time and generations long before their fathers, we see it as something pervasive and lasting: anything but an idiosyncrasy of a man or a group. Not as something that sometimes happens and is of no consequence. I quoted just now Wittgenstein's: "by the thought of man and his past". Why has the "thought of his past" such importance?

4.   Whatever gives us the *impression* that a practice must be age-old – this is what is important. The actual tracing of its descent from a fire ritual of human sacrifice – once this has been established – is "uninteresting" or superfluous for the question Wittgenstein is asking. But he sees that Frazer and those who go his way have recognized something important about rituals, something which leads them to emphasize the history of a ritual and to recognize that a ritual as we watch or read of it now is a continuation or development of rituals in earlier times.

> There is one conviction that underlies [or is taken for granted in] the hypotheses about the origin of, say, the Beltane festival; namely that festivals of this kind are not so to speak haphazard inventions of one man but need an infinitely broader basis if they are to persist. If I tried to invent a festival it would very soon die out or else be so modified that it corresponded to a general inclination in people. (*The Human World*, p. 40)

If the people celebrating here are following a ritual, this generally has been handed down to them, and most of those taking part have grown up with it. If a ritual, like that of human sacrifice, were something anybody could *invent*, at least he must have lived long among the people to whom he proposed it; he must have known the chronicles and the traditions of their history and the songs – all the ways in which these people thought about the earlier history of their tribe or nation. Even then it would be hard to imagine.

At first sight a comment which Wittgenstein makes a little
later seems hard to square with this:

> All these *different* customs show that it is not a matter here of one
> thing's being derived from another, but of a spirit common to a
> number of things. A person might himself have invented or made
> up all these ceremonies. And the spirit in which one invented
> them would be the very same as the spirit common to them all.
> (*Synthese* 17, p. 251 [not translated in *The Human World*])

I do not think this means that any one of us could invent or make
up all these ceremonies without having studied ceremonies
which we did *not* invent; still less that any of the actual
ceremonies came into being on the directions of someone who
invented them. In the passage I quoted earlier (p. 98) Wittgenstein speaks of something like an "association of ideas" which
we might call an "association of practices". And this suggests the
sense in which he speaks here of inventing different ceremonies.
It would have analogy to 'inventing' variations on a musical
theme; but this is limited, and could mislead. The idea is that
what brings all these ritual practices together, so that we study
them from the same interest, is not that they have all come about
in the same way, or have a similar sort of ancestry; nor is it
because they are alike in any "external" features (which we
might describe or draw); it is because we can see a common
Geist (spirit, inward nature, character . . .) through all of them.
Wittgenstein refers to this when he says the Beltane festival (for
example) gives an impression not only of something deep but
also of something *sinister* (*finster*: the word has a stronger sense of
'dark' and of 'gloom' than 'sinister' does in English; but it does
mean 'sinister' in the sense in which gloom or obscurity may be
sinister).
  He explains the phrase "the spirit of the festival" when he asks
(on page 38) if what we find sinister in the Beltane fire-festival
celebrated by the Scottish children in the eighteenth century is

something to do with the festival itself, or whether we shall find it sinister only if the conjecture that it originated in human sacrifice has been well established. His answer is:

> I think it is clear that what gives us a sinister impression is the *inner nature* of the practice as performed in recent times . . . When I speak of the inner nature of the practice I mean *all those circumstances* in which it is carried out *that are not included in the account* of the festival, *because they consist not* so much *in particular actions* which characterize it, but rather in what we might call the spirit of the festival: *which would be described by, for example, describing the sort of people* that take part, *their way of behaviour at other times*, i.e. their character, and *the other kinds of games that they play*. And we should then see that what is sinister lies in the character of these people themselves. (RR's italics throughout)

What in other passages he calls the "evidence" or the "grounds" for taking this to be a survival from a practice of human sacrifice, would count among those "circumstances" which give us the *Geist*, the "inner nature" of the festival. The phrase "inner nature" here is akin to, say, "the inner life of thought and feeling"; neither need be mysterious.

So far, this does not explain "a spirit *common* to all these ceremonies". But we can find this in two remarks I quoted earlier (p. 100). He had asked whether the thought that the casting of lots by drawing bits of cake from a hat was once a step in the sacrifice of a human being, whether this *thought* was not enough to explain the uneasy and sinister impression we have. And he answered, "Yes, but what I find in those accounts is something they have from the *evidence* or grounds for that thought — including evidence that does not seem directly connected with it: from reflecting on men, mankind and the past of mankind, on all that is queer (and dangerous to meddle with) which I see in myself and see and have seen and heard in others." This helps to explain the other passage, in which he says that what is disturbing in the idea of human sacrifice is just as obscure and perplexing as the impression we get from the accounts of the celebration and the burning of a straw man in eighteenth-century Scotland. What is deep and sinister about this celebration by the children does not become clear and obvious if all we are told is the origin and history of the external movements performed in it; "No, . . . *we* impute it from an experience in ourselves." "An experience in ourselves": this is what we have observed in our own selves and what we have observed and heard in our concourse with others, the strangeness. . . .

He had said of the Beltane festival as "played" by the children, that when it is clear that what we find sinister belongs to the spirit of the festival, and when we reflect on all those circumstances that show it, "we should then see that what is sinister lies in the character of these people themselves"; that is, in the character of those who make up the community in which it is performed as well as those who take part in it. But the other reflections place it in ourselves and the rest of mankind. This may be clearer when we see what it does for the remark about inventing all these ceremonies.

Wittgenstein has said:

1   In all these practices we see something that is similar, at any rate, to the association of ideas and related to it. We could speak of an association of practices. (*The Human World*, p. 37)

2   All these *different* customs show that it is not a matter here of one thing's being derived from another, but of a spirit common to a number of things. A person might himself have invented or made up all these ceremonies. And the spirit in which one invented them would be the very same as the spirit common to them all.

3   There is one conviction that underlies the hypotheses about the origin of the Beltane festival, namely that they are not what you might call one man's haphazard inventions but need an infinitely broader basis if they are to persist. *If I tried to invent a*

festival it would very soon die out or else be so modified that it corresponded to some general propensity in people.

'A general inclination in people' is not the same as 'the spirit common to all these ceremonies'. If I could imagine a ritual practice for any *one* tribe or nation, it would have to fit in with some inclination that was general or universal among the people of that tribe, in earlier times as well as in the present. The external form of the ritual, the external actions and movements in it, would have to be (or become) something to which nearly everyone in this tribe would feel inclined. For it is the *external* actions or the external form of the festival, which that remark emphasizes: that which makes *this* festival so noticeably different from any other. The *Geist* of the festival is not external in this sense. When Wittgenstein says it is common to all the different practices and different ceremonies, this is not like describing a general form that is common to a variety of dances (call them square dances) as though it might be formulated in such a way as to provide for the special varieties of it.

Suppose someone said, "There might also be a ritual of *this* sort (naming various features it might have)." He would be guided in this by what he knows of actual rituals, those he has seen or heard described. And the 'invention' would come 'by association' – "Association of customs, or of ceremonies". (This is an awkward phrase if we go on to think: 'association by similarity', where this means similarity of *form* between one ceremony and another.) We might say that what is common (*gemeinsam*) is the 'medium' in which a description of ceremonies actually seen may lead me to imagine others: but the condition of this is that I know this same spirit in myself. "The spirit in which one invented them would be the very same as the spirit common to them all." Otherwise I could not understand what they were, nor imagine them.

Wittgenstein in relation to his Times

G. H. von Wright

1. It is a commonplace that Wittgenstein's impact on contemporary thinking has been at least as great as that of any other single philosopher of the twentieth century. He is, with Ernst Mach and Bertrand Russell, the spiritual father of the powerful movement of thought, known as logical positivism or logical empiricism, of which a great deal of what is nowadays cultivated under the names of philosophical logic and foundation research in mathematics and the theory of science may be considered an heir. This influence has stemmed mainly from the *Tractatus* or, rather, from interpretations put on that work by others. Wittgenstein's later thoughts inspired a trend which is often called "ordinary language philosophy" and which had its heyday in Oxford and some other universities in the English-speaking world in the 1950s and early 1960s. Wittgenstein's influence today is felt with increasing intensity in many quarters but is more implicit and indirect and therefore difficult to characterize in a uniform manner. Broadly speaking, one can notice an alienation of this influence from the typical logico-analytical philosophy and an affiliation of it to thinking in the traditions of phenomenology, hermeneutics, and even Hegelianism. The unravelling and evaluation of the various forms which Wittgenstein's influence has assumed will constitute a major chapter in the history, yet to be written, of twentieth-century philosophy and ideas.

2. It is, however, well known that Wittgenstein himself strongly repudiated his own influence. He saw in it, on the

whole, either distortion and misunderstanding or empty use of a catching jargon. I should like to tell a story here which I hope nobody will think malicious. In the mid-1940s appeared an able and also very influential book with the title —— *and Language*. Its author had for a long time studied with Wittgenstein at Cambridge – and the two got on very well together. When I expressed astonishment at how little this book, in my opinion, owed to him, Wittgenstein said in his striking and inimitable manner that all this author had learned from him was "and Language". I think this characterization holds good for much, or most, of the work in contemporary philosophy for which Wittgenstein's teaching or published writings have been a source of inspiration. It is surely part of Wittgenstein's achievement to have made concern for language central to philosophy. But few only of those whom Wittgenstein made have this concern shared the peculiar motivation which *he* had for it. *One* aspect of Wittgenstein's all too obvious alienation from his times is his feeling that not even those who professed to follow him were really engaged in the same spiritual endeavour with him.

Wittgenstein also had grave doubts whether he was a good teacher. In 1940 he wrote:

> A teacher may get good, even astounding, results from his pupils while he is teaching them and yet not be a good teacher; because it may be that, while his pupils are directly under his influence, he raises them to a height which is not natural to them, without fostering their own capacities for work at this level, so that they immediately decline again as soon as the teacher leaves the classroom. (*Culture and Value*, p. 38)

To these facts about Wittgenstein's attitude to his own influence and teaching one can react by asking two questions. The first is: Why should one feel Wittgenstein's repudiation of his influence disturbing? This influence has been and continues to be a

seminal factor in philosophy, and *this* is what is important, not
how faithfully it reflects the intentions and the spirit of its
originator. These latter things must remain a matter of conjecture and it is not at all certain that speculating about them is
philosophically rewarding. I do not wish to dispute this. But I
would claim that trying to understand Wittgenstein in relation
to his times is a task in its own right, not to be dismissed as either
idle or irrelevant. It may not be relevant to the philosophy of
others; but it is certainly relevant to understanding the
philosophy of Wittgenstein.

The second question I had in mind is whether Wittgenstein's
attitude to his contemporaries is at all unique. What was the
reaction of other great philosophers? Did not all of them feel
that they were ahead of their times and therefore could not be
properly understood until an entirely new climate of opinion
had come to prevail? How did Plato or Descartes or Kant or
Hegel feel about this? I do not think that we have enough
evidence for a safe answer to these questions. Plato and Hegel
were in any case magisterial teachers. Descartes did not teach
but he lived in intense intellectual communication with the
avant-garde of his time. Kant's case is perhaps a little more like
Wittgenstein's. But I still think that Wittgenstein's attitude to
his time makes him unique among the great philosophers – and I
shall try to say something here to substantiate this claim.

3. In remarks from late in his life Wittgenstein wrote: "I
cannot found a school because I do not really want to be imi-
tated" (*Culture and Value*, p. 61). And: "I am by no means sure
that I should prefer a continuation of my work by others to a
change in the way people live which would make all these
questions superfluous." (*ibid.*) Wittgenstein thus thought that the
problems with which he was struggling were somehow connected with "the way people live", that is, with features of our
culture or civilization to which he and his pupils belonged. His
attitude to this culture was, as we shall see, one of censure and
even disgust. He therefore wished these ways of life changed,

but he had no faith that he or his teaching would change them. One day, however, there will be another culture with different patterns (*Culture and Value*, p. 64). Then, he says, the questions which had tormented him simply will not arise.

In order to see how Wittgenstein could think thus, one must first note that it was his philosophic conviction that the life of the human individual and therefore also all individual manifestations of culture are deeply entrenched in basic structures of a *social* nature. The structures in question are what Wittgenstein calls "*Lebensformen*", forms of life, and their embodiment in what he calls "*Sprachspiele*", language-games; they are "*das Hinzunehmende, Gegebene*", that which we accept in all our judging and thinking (cf. *Philosophical Investigations*, p. 226; *On Certainty*, §559). This basis, to be sure, is not eternal and immutable. It is a product of human history and changes with history. It is something man made and *he* changes. But *how* this happens is, according to Wittgenstein, not to be accounted for by a theory, or foreseen. "Who knows the laws according to which society develops?" he asks, and adds, "I am quite sure they are a closed book even to the cleverest of men." (*Culture and Value*, p. 60)

4. Wittgenstein's view of the entrenchment of the individual in social reality is intimately connected with his view of the nature of philosophy. The problems of philosophy have their root in a distortion or malfunctioning of the language-games which in its turn signalizes that something is wrong with the ways in which men live. On the intellectual level this malfunctioning consists in certain unhealthy habits of thought ("*Denkgewohnheiten*"), permeating the intellectual culture of a time.

Wittgenstein's philosophizing can to a great extent be seen as a fight against such thought-habits (cf. *Culture and Value*, p. 44). This is perhaps most strikingly true of his philosophy of mathematics. It fights the influence of set theory on foundation research and on thinking about the subject. It is true also of the second main branch of his work, the philosophy of psychology. But here the situation is more complex in that Wittgenstein wages a war on two fronts: against behaviourism on the one hand and against mentalism on the other.

It is against this background that we must understand why Wittgenstein, in the midst of writing about set theory and the notion of the actual infinite, should have written down the often-quoted remark:

> The sickness of a time is cured by an alteration in the mode of life of human beings, and it was possible for the sickness of philosophical problems to get cured only through a changed mode of thought and of life, not through a medicine invented by an individual. – Suppose the use of the motor-car produces or encourages certain illnesses, and mankind is plagued by such illness until, from some cause or other, as the result of some development or other, it abandons the habit of driving. (*Remarks on the Foundations of Mathematics*, p. 57)

The phrase is impressive even when quoted out of context. But it gets a new dimension when we read it in the context where it stands. To Wittgenstein set theory was a cancer rooted deep in the body of our culture and with distorting effects on that part of our culture which is our mathematics. Had he lived to see the role which set theory has since come to play in many or most countries as a basis for teaching mathematics to children he would no doubt have felt disgusted and perhaps have said that it signalized the end of what used to be known as mathematics.

5. The habits of thought Wittgenstein is fighting are not, however, primarily the unwholesome influence on our thinking of certain lofty intellectual creations, such as Cantor's. Set theory or behaviouristic psychology are only symptoms of a sickness, not its cause. The cause is in the language-games and reflects in its turn the way of life.

It is vain to think that by fighting the symptoms one can cure the illness. Curing it would mean changing the language-games, reforming language – and therewith the community's way of thought and life. Wittgenstein certainly did not think this possible through the efforts of an individual. He is most emphatic about that. All the philosopher can do is to expose the disorder in the language-games, describe it, and thereby rid his mind of the torments produced by the unrecognized illness. But this intellectual cure – "Thoughts that are at peace" which, he says (*Culture and Value*, p. 43), is the aim of philosophy – will have no important consequences of a social nature, either for habits of thinking or for way of life.

Wittgenstein's attitude to language, therefore, is a fighting but not a reformist attitude. "We are struggling with language. We are engaged in a struggle with language", he writes (*Culture and Value*, p. 11). What he means can be further elucidated by a passage of about the same date, the early 1930s, which is not printed in *Culture and Value* because it is inseparable from other things he then writes about the nature of philosophy:

> Human beings are deeply embedded in philosophical – i.e. grammatical – confusions. Freeing them from these *presupposes* tearing them away from the enormous number of connecting links that hold them fast. A sort of rearrangement of the whole of their language is needed. – But of course that language has developed the way it has because some human beings felt – and still feel – inclined to think that way. So the tearing away will succeed only with those in whose life there already is an instinctive revolt against the language in question and not with those whose whole instinct is for life in the very herd which created that language as its proper expression. (MS 213, 423)

6. When Wittgenstein wrote the above he perhaps did not see as clearly as he did later the connection between language and ways of life. In the perspective of his later philosophy one could say that his "revolt against language" was a renunciation

("*Abstandnahme*"), the marking of a distance from the complex web of forms of life ("*Lebensformen*"), which constitute contemporary Western civilization.

Wittgenstein's life testifies to this. So too did his words, not only in conversation but also in what he wrote, most explicitly perhaps in the printed preface to *Philosophical Remarks* and its different drafts in the manuscripts. The spirit in which he is writing, he says, is "different from the one which informs the vast stream of European and American civilization in which all of us stand". The spirit of this civilization is to him "alien and uncongenial" ("*fremd und unsympathisch*") (*Culture and Value*, p. 6). Its hallmark is belief in progress (p. 7) – progress above all thanks to the technological applications of science. Wittgenstein deeply distrusted it. Many readers must have been puzzled by the motto for *Philosophical Investigations*: "It is a thing about progress: it generally looks bigger than it really is." If one reads it in its context in Nestroy's play, *Der Schützling*, one will perhaps understand it better. Progress, we are there told, is only the greening fringe of a colonial territory with a vast hinterland of impenetrable wilderness. In 1947 Wittgenstein wrote:

> It isn't absurd, e.g., to believe that the age of science and technology is the beginning of the end for humanity; that the idea of great progress is a delusion, along with the idea that the truth will ultimately be known; that there is nothing good or desirable about scientific knowledge and that mankind, in seeking it, is falling into a trap. It is by no means obvious that this is not how things are. (*Culture and Value*, p. 56)

Wittgenstein calls this the "apocalyptic view of the world". A little later Wittgenstein wrote:

> Science and industry, and their progress, might turn out to be the most enduring thing in the modern world. Perhaps any speculation about a coming collapse of science and industry is, for the

present and for a *long* time to come, nothing but a dream; perhaps science and industry, having caused infinite misery in the process, will unite the world – I mean condense it into a *single* unit, though one in which peace is the last thing that will find a home.

Because science and industry do decide wars, or so it seems. (*ibid.*, p. 63)

Had Wittgenstein lived to see the sixties and seventies of our century he would, no doubt, have found plenty to reinforce his view of the dangers of self-destruction inherent in the nature of modern industrial society.

These gloomy prospects notwithstanding, Wittgenstein's world view is anything but "prophetic". It has no vision of the future; rather it has a touch of nostalgia about the past. Wittgenstein did not feel himself like Nietzsche "a shaft of longing for the opposite shore" ("*ein Pfeil der Sehnsucht nach dem andern Ufer*"), since this would have presupposed a vision of a distant shore on which shipwrecked man could start a new life. For Wittgenstein the future was something unforeseeable. He has several remarks relating to this topic. "You can't *build* clouds. And that's why the future you *dream* of never comes true", he writes (*Culture and Value*, p. 41).

When we think of the world's future, we always mean the destination it will reach if it keeps going in the direction we can see it going in now; it does not occur to us that its path is not a straight line but a curve, constantly changing direction. (*ibid.*, p. 3)

The philosopher who thinks thus not only makes no forecasts, he is also under no illusion that there will be a continuation to the work he himself began but was perhaps not able to complete (*Culture and Value*, p. 25; cf. also p. 61).

7.   Many readers will no doubt be struck by the strongly Spenglerian nature of Wittgenstein's attitude to his times. The observation would perhaps not be very interesting, were it not

for the fact that Wittgenstein's outlook is intimately allied to his philosophy. Wittgenstein did not, like Spengler, develop a philosophy of history. But he *lived* the *"Untergang des Abendlandes"*, the decline of the West, one could say. He lived it, not only in his disgust for contemporary Western civilization, but also in his deep awe and understanding of this civilization's' great past. How else could he have written these words which I find deeply moving: "The earlier culture will become a heap of rubble and finally a heap of ashes, but spirits will hover over the ashes" (*Culture and Value*, p. 3).

Since these affinities with Spengler may not be familiar to many, and may strike some people as strange, the matter requires some further documentation. The fact is that Wittgenstein *was* influenced by Spengler. There is a passage in *Culture and Value* (p. 19) where he mentions those who had influenced him. It is worth giving the list in full here: Boltzmann, Hertz, Schopenhauer, Frege, Russell, Kraus, Loos, Weininger, Spengler, Sraffa. This is Wittgenstein's order of enumeration and I think it answers to the chronological order of influence. The remark was written in 1931 but I doubt whether Wittgenstein would have added to the list later in life.

It is not certain, however, that Wittgenstein in the passage referred to meant that Spengler had influenced his view of life; it is rather that Spengler's work had reinforced and helped him to articulate his view. The actual influence pertains, it seems, to an idea in Wittgenstein's later philosophy, indeed to one of its most characteristic thought manoeuvres. This is the idea of "family resemblance". It appears to have its origin in Spengler's notion of the *Ur-symbol* which characterizes each one of the great cultures and constitutes what Wittgenstein, writing about this, in fact calls "a family resemblance" (*Culture and Value*, p. 14) between a culture's various manifestations – its mathematics, architecture, religion, social and political organization, and so forth. The decay of a culture is, in many ways, a dissolution of the resemblances which unite its ways of

life, with, as Wittgenstein puts it, "the best men all contributing
to the same great end", instead of, as "in an age without culture,
when they work for purely private ends" (*Culture and Value*,
p. 6).

8. Few ideas have been more grossly misunderstood and
vulgarized than the Spenglerian notion of an "*Untergang des
Abendlandes*". People tend to identify it with a prophecy of im-
pending disaster – something like an earthquake or deluge. It is
not this. Nor is it a forecast of war or of an ecological crisis due
to man's thoughtless exploitation of nature – though both surely
are features accompanying the decline of the West, just as they
were characteristic of the vanishing of the Greco-Roman
culture preceding ours. The perspective of decline, *Untergang*, is
what Wittgenstein, speaking of Spengler, calls a "principle
determining the form of one's reflections" ("*Prinzip der
Betrachtungsform*") or a "form of discussion" (*Culture and Value*,
p. 27, 14). And he criticizes Spengler for a tendency to confuse
the *Urbild*, or type, the "object of comparison . . . from which
this way of viewing things is derived" with the "object we are
viewing in its light" (*ibid*., p. 14). One cannot speak of true and
false as attributes of a way of viewing things, a *Betrachtungsweise*.
But it gets its significance, of course, from the phenomena it
illuminates, and its justification from how much it contributes
to our understanding of history.

To many people this way of viewing things is simply unintelligible; others will find it artificial or exaggerated. Its
appeal for those who find it natural will depend partly on
features of character and temperament, partly on background
and traditions, partly on experience in life. It is surely deeply
significant of the formation of Wittgenstein's view of contemporary civilization that he grew up in the strangely
contradiction-loaded melting-pot of nations and ideas which
was the late Hapsburg empire and that during his life-time he
suffered the barbarism which extinguished that peculiar ferment
of our culture which was represented by Central European

Jewry. (Reflections on the Jewish mind are abundant in *Culture and Value*.)

Wittgenstein was deeply rooted in something which became completely uprooted; in order to appreciate the way he saw the world one must understand this double aspect of tradition and rupture with the past which affected his own life.

9. I have dwelt here on three aspects of Wittgenstein's thought; on two of them quite briefly because they are familiar and on the third which is less well known at some length. The first is the view that the individual's beliefs, judgements, and thoughts are entrenched in unquestioningly accepted language-games and socially sanctioned forms of life. The second is the view that philosophical problems are disquietudes of the mind caused by some malfunctioning in the language-games and hence in the way of life of the community. The third is Wittgenstein's rejection of the scientific-technological civilization of industrialized societies, which he regarded as the decay of a culture.

It can hardly be denied that these three aspects are closely interconnected and deeply integrated in Wittgenstein's intellectual personality. An effort to understand it which does not pay due attention to this fact is doomed to failure. What is problematic, however, is whether or to what extent the three aspects are separable from one another in thought or whether there is also some kind of conceptual connectedness between them. Particularly pertinent is the question whether the third aspect, the Spenglerian one, is only contingently, that is for historical and psychological reasons, connected with the other two in Wittgenstein's thought. If the connection is only accidental or contingent, then one could say that Wittgenstein's attitude to his times is irrelevant to the understanding of his philosophy, even though it may be quite important to an understanding of his personality.

I wish I knew how to answer these questions. To me they pose a problem. If it were only a question of the relation between the first and the third aspect – the entrenchment of individual life in social reality on the one hand and the rejection of contemporary civilization on the other hand – the matter would be easy. There is not much reason for thinking that *they* are connected. The difficulty arises because of the second aspect, Wittgenstein's peculiar view of the nature of philosophy. It constitutes a link between the two other aspects. Because of the interlocking of language and ways of life, a disorder in the former reflects disorder in the latter. If philosophic problems are symptomatic of language producing malignant outgrowths which obscure our thinking, then there must be a cancer in the *Lebensweise*, in the way of life itself.

I do not think that Wittgenstein would have claimed that his conception of philosophy was valid for all the historical phenomena which we heap under the label 'philosophy'. It is a well-known saying of his that what he did was "a legitimate heir" related by family resemblance to what philosophers of the past had done. Philosophy is not a "historical constant", any more than science or art are. Wittgenstein is much more deeply "history-conscious" than is commonly recognized and understood. His way of seeing philosophy was not an attempt to tell us what philosophy, once and for all, *is* but expressed what for him, in the setting of his times, it had to be.

If Wittgenstein had claimed a non-historical, timeless validity for his view of philosophy, then again there could be nothing more than a psychological connection between it and his attitude to his times. Because then the claim would entail that good philosophy went with decline in culture. This is obviously wrong: the great philosophies mark the peak of a culture, or at most the beginning of its decline. But Wittgenstein made no such claim. His conception of philosophy is intimately allied to a way of viewing contemporary civilization. This much we must concede. But whether this had to be the Spenglerian form of seeing our times as a dissolution of those traditions in art, religion, science, and philosophy which had constituted the relative unity of the historical phenomenon of Western culture is, of course, another matter. Whatever the answer, the question deserves to be thought about and belongs to a so far almost unexplored problem area which Wittgenstein bequeathed to philosophy.

Index